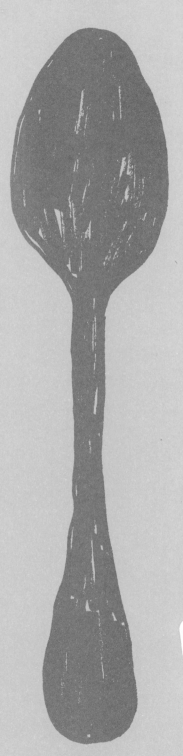

HEARTLANDIA

HERITAGE RECIPES FROM PORTLAND'S
THE COUNTRY CAT

HEARTLANDIA

ADAM AND JACKIE SAPPINGTON

WITH ASHLEY GARTLAND

PHOTOGRAPHY BY JOHN VALLS

Houghton Mifflin Harcourt

Boston New York 2015

Copyright © 2015 by Adam Sappington and Jackie Sappington
Interior photography © 2015 by John Valls
Additional photographs (pages 10–11) © 2015 by Debbie Baxter

For information about permission to reproduce selections from this book, write to
Permissions, Houghton Mifflin Harcourt Publishing Company,
215 Park Avenue South, New York, New York 10003.

www.hmhco.com

Library of Congress Cataloging-in-Publication Data
Sappington, Adam.
Heartlandia : heritage recipes from the Country Cat /
Adam and Jackie Sappington with Ashley Gartland.
pages cm
Includes index.
ISBN 978-0-544-36377-9 (hardcover) —
ISBN 978-0-544-36378-6 (ebook)
1. Country Cat Dinner House & Bar (Portland, Ore.)
2. Cooking, American.
I. Sappington, Jackie.
II. Gartland, Ashley.
III. Title.
TX715.S145246 2015
641.5973—dc23 2014036933

Book design by Jennifer S. Muller

Printed in China
C&C 10 9 8 7 6 5 4 3 2 1

To Atticus and Quinn, you are our heart and soul. We love
you more than words can say. Work hard, never give up, and
follow your dreams.

To Josh–you will be sorely missed.

CONTENTS

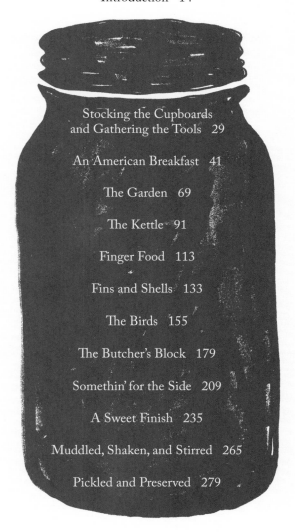

FOREWORD

I love America, I guess, and the food that supposedly represents it—the high-piled platters of fried chicken, served alongside overflowing bowls of viscous gravy; thick and burnished slices of bacon, sizzling their lives away in an ancient black pan; plump, jet-black berries, spilling out from ethereally flaky pie crusts. You hear a lot about those dishes, and see them in magazines, but how often do you really get to eat them? I know them better as ideals, something I see in a documentary celebrating some shriveled but saucy crone somewhere. They struck me as something of a sham, the front end of a bait-and-switch with me eating instant grits. Then I went to Portland one day, and in a corner restaurant in an out-of-the-way neighborhood, my faith came back to me.

The food that Adam and Jackie Sappington cook at The Country Cat, whatever you may have heard, does not in fact pay tribute to the past. It doesn't reference forgotten foodways, or pass on lessons learned in Grandmother's kitchen. Anyway, it doesn't try to do that. And because it doesn't try, the Sappingtons are able, like few people in America, to escape the trap of time and bring the old cooking, uncorrupted and unstylized, into 2015. If Adam Sappington's grandmother were alive and working the line at The Country Cat, she would be cooking hard and fast, and thinking of ways to make her roast pork better, and keeping it warm for the last turn of customers. Like Adam, she, too, would no doubt be using the food that is close at hand, whether or not it fits in any particular established style. My favorite memory of him involves no cooking at all; I was in a kitchen amphitheater, waiting to do a burger demo, when he showed up with a zipper bag, looking for all the world like a back-country drug dealer, whispering to me to "check this out." He opened the bag a crack to give me a whiff. I naturally expected a heady whiff of cannabis; instead, I got hit with the earthy perfume of freshly dug yellowfoot chanterelles, mushrooms he had picked a couple of hours earlier in the countryside. He grinned like a guy who thought he had the world by the tail. I think maybe he does.

The other thing I like about that story is not the way it expresses his enthusiasm for local ingredients, which every chef in the world shares, or claims to share; it's that his excitement centered on something so perishable and unexotic, something that cost nothing and required no particular skill to use. His feelings about those mushrooms were personal; they had nothing to do with him as a chef. And those are the feelings I think most define The Country Cat's character. It isn't Adam's past or background that really matters; he would be just as good a cook if he were Belgian.

No, what matters at The Country Cat, for all the greatness of its food, are the emotions that brought it into existence and maintained it through some very lean years. Two people who love each other and who love food opened a restaurant with a trippy logo and a modern menu, and served punk rockers and potheads, and strived to make them happy in this particular time and place, the best way they knew how. The connection to an older, more rural America wasn't the point; but again, it was there, and it was powerful. It made me feel a vicarious connection to a place and time that was completely alien to me. I feel—and I think all the Cat's customers feel—a kind of distant familial connection to it, like long-lost relations finding our way back to a home we never had. What do I have to do with Mother Sappington? My people come from Minsk, not Missouri, and would be horrified if they saw the way I gobble down ham and bacon at the Cat's bar, chasing it with small-batch whiskey and talking to the servers about their abundant tattoos. But for all their disapproval, I think my forebears would be moved by how much feeling holds the place together, and they'd be happy to see that I was part of a community, one bound by loyalty and bourbon and biscuits.

That community starts with the Sappingtons, but it doesn't end with them. The old Southern foodways were as much social as culinary; as their eulogists are so fond of saying, big meals were one of the things that brought people together. That much carries over to the very real, very specific place where Jackie and Adam started their restaurant. The people of Portland cohere famously around cafes and bars; but most of all, they love restaurants. Montavilla, the sleepy northern neighborhood where the Cat is found, is unquestionably its center. There is a three- or four-block stretch of Stark Street that is the nerve center of neighborhood. There is a blue-collar sports bar that makes fine cheesesteaks across the street; around the corner, another, cooler spot caters to cooler types. There

is an old movie theater that shows new movies on old screens, and serves beer and wine; an eclectic, sunny café; a couple of thrift shops; and one or two other places. But it is at the corner of Eightieth and Stark that the action can be found, where the lights shine out the brightest, where the murmur of expectant and satisfied customers come and go, and where frequently whole families stand in the street waiting to get in. They don't mind, because it's worth it. If Adam and Jackie didn't own the place, I have no doubt that they and their kids would wait outside themselves, because a great meal is always worth waiting for, and because a neighborhood has to support its own.

But now The Country Cat has gained national fame. TV hosts go there to gawk at Adam's chicken. I even went so far as to move all the way from New York just to be closer to it; when I moved to Portland, one of Adam's signature fried chicken–and–martinis parties marked the occasion, and welcomed me to the neighborhood. Now that you have this book, you should consider yourself at least peripherally part of it as well. The book is called *Heartlandia*, but it isn't to some imaginary middle America that the name refers; to me at least, it's the open heart of the Sappingtons and the people around them, all bound in gravy and the milk of human kindness. I don't know what people ate a hundred years ago, and a hundred years from now, we may be fed by robots; but right here, right now, The Country Cat is open for business, the very heart of what American food is like at its generous best.

—Josh Ozersky, Editor at Large, *Esquire*

ACKNOWLEDGMENTS

Heartlandia is not just about the food from our restaurant, The Country Cat Dinner House & Bar. The taste memories of the foods we have shared and prepared with our mothers, our grandmothers, our friends, and family also drive this book. With that said, we have so many people to thank for helping us get this labor of love on the shelf.

The inspiration to get our recipes and stories on paper wouldn't have happened without the help of our collaborator, Ashley Gartland. She continually kept us on deadline and on track and always asked us the tough questions. To John and Theresa Valls: Thank you for styling and shooting beautiful photographs that brought the story and recipes to life. To Debbie Baxter, for shooting terrific portraits of us. Thanks to our agent, Betsy Amster, who has been a wonderful guide, listener, and mentor throughout this process. She always made time for us as we waded through the daunting task of writing a book.

A huge thank-you to our editor, Justin Schwartz; his assistant, Cynthia Brzostowski; art director, Melissa Lotfy; and copy editor, Ivy McFadden, at Houghton Mifflin Harcourt for giving us the chance and for believing in us to tell our story and share the recipes of our American heartland and The Country Cat. Thank you, thank you, thank you to Jennifer S. Muller for putting together a beautiful, lively book that truly reflects our voice and vision.

To our staff at The Country Cat, past and present. You have helped us carve out and create the soul of the restaurant on so many levels. Words can't quite describe our gratitude to our restaurant family: The Rilz, LAR, MC Eells, El Chignon, Smidgie Mitch, Meggie, Little Leah, KOJ, Ms. Madeline, Miss Leah Miller, Gonzo, Mule, Big B, Skeeter, Weffer, F-@%! B (Matthews), Breezers, El Presidente, Sanchez, Big Al, Cracker, Big J, Woody, Brian, Jenny Jenn, Nick, Dylan, Javier, Francisco, Jamie, Jess, McCaffery, Danika, Crystal, Kerry S., Duncan, Athena, Karen, Andrea, and everyone else who has passed through our doors.

We would be remiss if we did not mention the HUGE supporters of The Country Cat, our customers. Thank you for the years of support, your feedback, and your patronage!

A special thank-you to Megan Wortman of the American Lamb Board for all the support and belief in our mission statement and drive to use everything with lamb!

To Stephen Gerike of the Pork Board for being the "band leader" and bringing together all the "meat-heads" in the world!

Teri Rippito! You gave me the chance! Love you! And thank you.

To my brother, Big E! You dreamed up and captured the image and character of THE Country Cat and provide encouragement when we need it the most. You're the best, baby, and I love ya like a crazy man!!

Carrie, Jannie, and the Little Green Pickle PR crew!! Why you gotta be so good, baby? We love all that you do and all that you have done to constantly support us and listen. You always shoot the straight skinny.

Mr. Mike Thelin. You have always believed in and spoken the gospel of what The Country Cat stands for. You have helped in so many ways to put our ass on the map. You are a true gentleman and one of our closest friends. Thank you for shining a light on what we do and how we do it, brother.

Jeff and Scott, thank you for being protective big brothers who always have my back. Your support in our endeavors has meant so much!

Oh, Art, you are a lifesaver in so many ways! Thank you for always being a phone call away!

Mr. Marvin T.! The man among men! Thank you for all you have done and all that you do!

For that ol' gyall of mine, Robyn "Ly" Lively Johnson, my BFF and soul sister: You and your family gave me my first exposure to down-home, heartland, family cookin' and helped spur my love affair with American heritage cooking and history in many ways.

To our recipe testers Shirleen Bakken, Danielle Centoni, Louisa Neumann, Kris and Ryan Furst, Lauren and Alex Umbdenstock, Megen Pullen, Garrett Berdan, Jake Gartland, Nancy Lynn Jones, and Holly Scholar: Thank you for taking the time to read through, cook, and comment on the recipes. Your work and feedback was so important and appreciated.

To the wonderful Woo family, thanks for being willing to be photographed while you eat! You guys rock!!

Thank you, Josh Ozersky, for wanting to write our foreword even before we'd written the book. You are the MAN and a true preserver of the history of American heritage cooking.

Cory Schreiber, thanks for being our mentor, our sounding board, and one of the trailblazers who shared the importance of knowing your local farmer, rancher, and fishmonger.

Aunt Ronda, thank you for traveling to Missouri and retelling the story of Granny Cris, your sister Gramma Gina, and the magic of the Crismon family's fried chicken legacy. These stories and my own memories have truly shaped my love for fried chicken and the heritage and history of heartland cooking.

And thanks to our mommas, Nancy and Holly, for always being our cheerleaders—even when you're scared to death of what we are doing. You have been nothing short of AMAZING, not to mention a massive support and rock whenever we needed to lean on you. You inspire us to keep moving forward to follow our dreams.

—Adam and Jackie

INTRODUCTION

I grew up in the heart of rural Missouri, which meant I ate a steady diet of biscuits, butter, and green beans braised to the point of perfection. At my family table, we ate the foods of America's heartland: sugar bread and butter, iceberg lettuce and cucumber salads, Burgers' country ham, and, of course, fried chicken.

Nearly every meal was about the fried chicken. No one got tired of it—it was just what we ate. We served it at every family picnic, every holiday gathering, and every Sunday night, too. At the start of each week, we'd spread a pile of newspapers on the living room floor and eat Mom's fried chicken, mashed potatoes and gravy, coleslaw, and biscuits, picnic-style. There was sun tea for my mom and martinis for my pop because he always said nothing goes better with fried chicken than gin. He loved to prove his point by letting me have a little nip of his martini when I was young.

I liked listening to classic rock and floating down the river as much as any Midwest boy, but I also spent a lot of time helping my mom and grannies shop for ingredients and cook our food. My mom was all about going to the supermarket but my gramma Gina, well, she knew where to get the special stuff. We'd drive down to the little league baseball fields together and watch the farmers pull up in their trucks and open their beds to sell their wares. You knew you were in Missouri because those truck beds were full of beefsteak tomatoes, corn, and tons of green beans. We'd buy what looked good and fresh and head back to the kitchen, where we would pull out a brown paper bag, pour out the beans, and start picking.

By the time I hit nineteen, I'd worked a few front-of-house restaurant gigs and really fallen in love with the professional side of cooking. So I applied for a job at this semi-progressive farm-to-table Italian restaurant that was a real revelation for rural Missouri. The labor pool was poor and the owner was probably looking for anyone who gave a shit, so she hired me to start cooking on the grill. I got my ass handed to me that first night, and again and again after that. I was hooked.

The work was hard but I quickly fell in love with the physicality of cooking and the soul of a working kitchen. I couldn't sleep after my shifts because I was so jacked up and stoked to learn more. So when this girl I was going with said she was looking to leave Missouri, we made a deal: We'd move to a place where she could get her master's degree and I could go to culinary school. We picked Portland, Oregon, sight unseen, packed up our stuff, and drove across the country to start our new lives.

Our son Quinn under the Missouri River Bridge | An old schoolhouse in mid-Missouri

JEFFERSON CITY, MISSOURI

The old train station in Jefferson City | An homage to President Truman and Missouri on Aunt Ronda's cabin wall

Culinary school didn't give me the same buzz that restaurant work did, but it helped me get my foot in the door at one of Portland's top restaurants, Wildwood. I started there as a culinary school extern and worked my way up to executive chef. It was over my ten-year tenure there that I learned how to prepare seasonal American food that represented the pure flavors of the region. Every day, our kitchen manager, Sam, would pull up to the restaurant with a truck full of fresh fruits and vegetables and introduce me to new ingredients like figs and fresh artichokes. I'd never seen those foods in redneck Missouri, and they helped shape my style of cooking and my craft. At Wildwood, I started preparing food in a more thoughtful way than I ever had before.

But man, I missed the fried chicken from the old days.

Fortunately, during my time at Wildwood, I met a cook who got my obsessions with fried chicken and heartland cuisine. Jackie had a degree in the anthropology of food, a passion for down-home cooking, and an interest in historical cookbooks and Rotary Club recipe collections that rivaled my own. And the girl could cook. She was one of those driven, self-taught cooks who started catering family friends' parties as a teenager in Los Angeles. Then she honed her cooking skills working on the line and in the pastry kitchen at some of Portland's best restaurants.

By the time I ended my other relationship, Jackie and I had started courting each other with Bloody Mary lunches, old copies of the Kentucky Housewife cookbook, and long conversations about what defined true American cooking, from the dishes served at picnics and country gatherings to the foods we ate as kids.

When I hit my plateau at Wildwood, we decided it was time to open our own place, where I could re-create my family table and introduce everyone to the heritage cuisine we love to cook and eat. It was a given that we'd serve my secret skillet-fried chicken at our neighborhood joint, but we also knew our menu would reach beyond that blue-collar staple. At our restaurant, we would use our fine-dining training and fresh, local ingredients to make authentic heartland cuisine.

It took a while for us to find the right fit for our American place, but when we walked into the old Dickson Drugstore, we had a feeling that this was it—and it's always about the gut for us. The spot sat in a sleepy little pocket of Portland but it already had the feel of community built into it because it had been the neighborhood's drugstore, post office, soda fountain, and more for the past sixty years. It had an off-kilter ramp out front, the kind that reminded me of the entrances of old drugstores in Missouri, and an old-school Rx mosaic to the left of the front door. We added checkerboard floors, parlor

The Gasconade River, Vienna, MO

Mom and I in her kitchen by the Missouri River

lights, and wooden booths and created a restaurant that felt as old America as the recipes we would serve in it.

We called it The Country Cat Dinner House & Bar.

The Country Cat might be based in Portland, but its roots go all the way back to my Midwest childhood. At our restaurant and at home, we're all about heritage cooking. We serve updated versions of dishes from my relatives' recipe boxes like Judy, skillet-fried chicken, and asparagus casserole, alongside reimagined classics like smoked tomato soup, pecan spoonbread, and grilled lamb leg steaks with balsamic-braised figs. With each order of challah French toast, turkey tails with blue cheese dressing, or bourbon peach crumble pie, we're putting our own spin on heartland cuisine to prove it's not just about pork and potatoes.

When people ask us how we make rustic grub taste so damn good, we tell them we're really making glorified Gramma cuisine and that our tricks go back generations. Cooking inspired by heartland ingredients and American craft methods is steeped in time and tradition. As early pioneers began to move west, many discovered the fruitful soil and wide-open plains of the heartland and laid down their roots. They spent their days tilling their farms and working on their ranches, so having farm- and ranch-direct products available to cook with was just a way of life.

We feel it's important to know where your food is coming from. For us, that means every dish starts with the best ingredients. We get fresh ingredients from local farms and then we prepare them in the simplest ways possible because we want to taste the true flavors of each one. That's the wholesome, honest way I ate growing up, so that's how we cook today; it's also why we make pantry staples like ketchup and ranch dressing in a style that speaks to the true flavor of craft cooking better than anything you could buy.

At the restaurant, we're working with limited space—two six-foot prep tables and one nine-by-eleven-foot walk-in–but we still find ways to make everything from scratch. If you stepped into the kitchen, you'd see fluffy buttermilk biscuits getting nice and golden in the oven, housemade ketchup bubbling away on the stove, and half a cow waiting in the walk-in for its turn on my butcher block. We put up our own preserves, make gallons of our Bloody Mary mix from scratch, and cure country ham using a process that we borrowed from good old Thomas Jefferson, because it's the Country Cat way to make everything by hand.

Our restaurant is the kind of place where you can start any day with a plate of spring vegetable hash or slide onto a bar stool in the afternoon and nurse a pint while snacking on warm buttery pretzels and housemade beef jerky. You can come in at sundown, when the

Yuckin' it up with the boys on the line in the Country Cat kitchen

dining room really starts to jive, and discover why honest heartland cuisine like our Whole Hog plate and olive oil–braised green beans satisfies the stomach and the soul. Or you can just sit down at the chef's counter and eat a slice of apple pie. Heartland cooking is like that—it comes straight from the heart and brings people together to create memories at the table.

At The Country Cat, and now in this book, we're sharing our distinct style of heritage cooking. Whether you live in a big city high rise or a little country town, we hope this book encourages you to try our craft-driven approach to cooking and start sharing the flavors of the heartland with your family and friends at home.

—Adam and Jackie

...e to The Country Cat! Back in the day, the Dickson Drugstore had an old Rx sign sitting to ...of the front door. We replaced it with a mosaic of a cat that my brother, Eric, created for us.

Our badass cooks

Getting ready for Saturday night

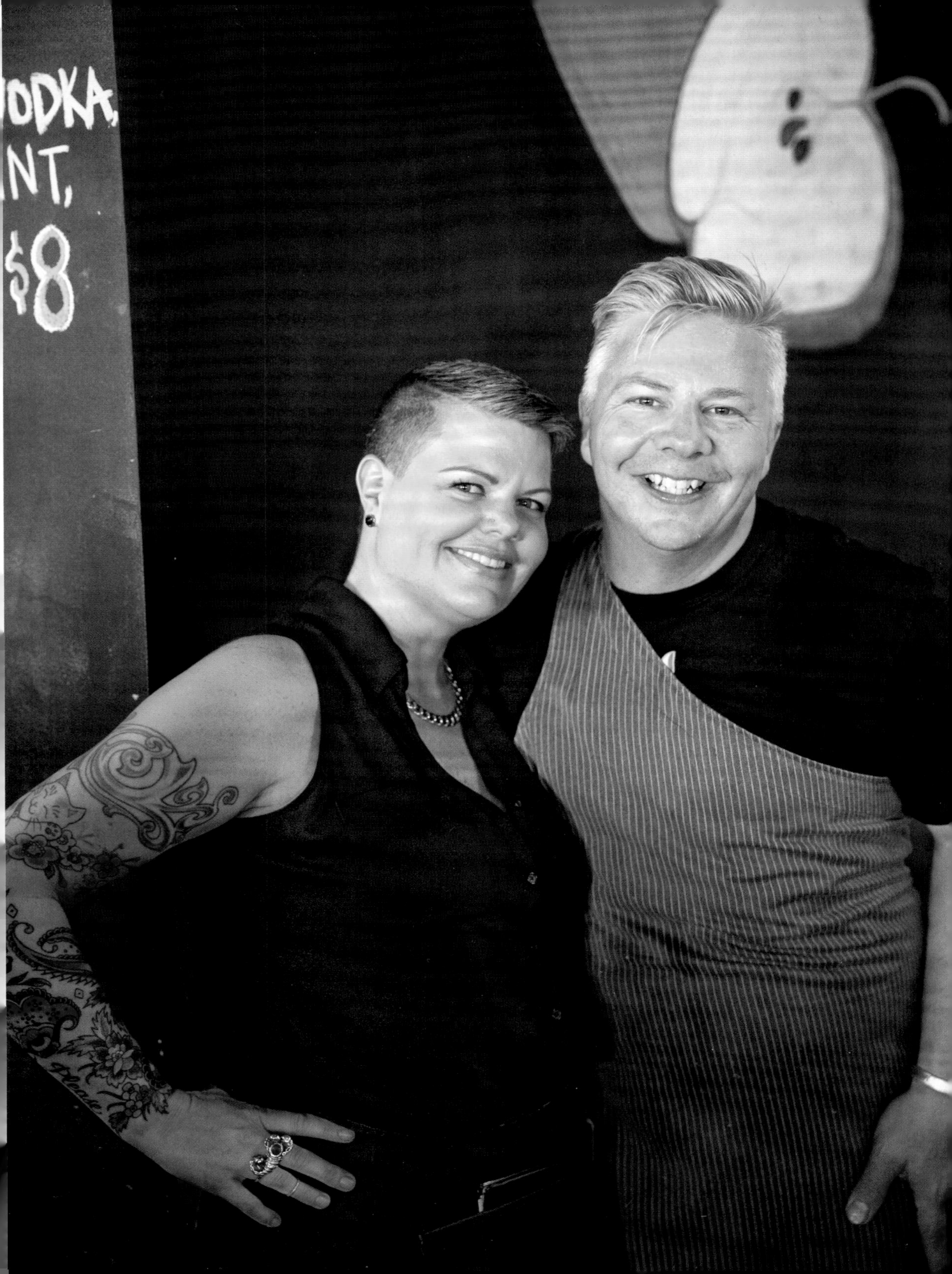
$8

STOCKING THE CUPBOARDS AND GATHERING THE TOOLS

Of the various tools, techniques, and ingredients used in our recipes, the most important one you'll need is common sense. Cooking takes time, care, and attention to the process and a willingness to trust your gut as much as what's written on the page in front of you. Recipes are really just roadmaps; use them to guide you through the steps to create something you'll want to feed yourself, your family, and your friends.

Start every recipe by reading the headnote and recipe instructions all the way through so you choose the right time to make the dish and get a successful result. Some of these recipes are fairly quick and easy to prepare, but others shouldn't be squeezed into a tight schedule or list of to-dos. Though both types of recipes will reward home cooks, we've included more involved recipes in each chapter for cooks who want to dig in and really learn the art of cooking from scratch. Taking the time to cook, cure, or preserve something the right way will lead to a different level of cooking and create flavors that have more depth and simply taste better.

Be sure to taste your dishes along the way. If you think something needs a little more of this or less of that, it's okay to change it. That's part of the fun—making a recipe your own by tweaking it here and there to suit your palate.

INGREDIENTS

You can find most of the ingredients we use in our cooking at a good grocery store or farmers' market. Here are a few favorites we consider key to building a Country Cat pantry. Stock up on these essentials, and our recipes will be within easy reach.

Aromatics

Aromatic vegetables like onions, garlic, leeks, fennel (also called anise), and shallots are exactly that—aromatic. They impart scent as well as flavor to any dish you use them in. I typically use them to build a flavor base in a myriad of dishes from soups to sauces to marinades.

You can easily grow aromatic vegetables in your garden or find them at grocery stores and farmers' markets. These vegetables should be stored in the refrigerator and used within two weeks to prevent spoilage. Unless I call for another type of onion specifically, I use yellow onions in my recipes. I like their neutral flavor—they aren't too strong or too sweet, and their nice, meaty texture can hold up to many different cooking techniques. In the spring, I love to use the first crops of young onions (also called spring onions), garlic, leeks, and fennel from local farms, as they are delicate in size and texture and provide a sweeter, milder flavor than the full-grown versions.

Fats

All fats are not created equal. The key to using fats is to use them in moderation and with purpose. When I add a particular fat to a dish, I consider its flavor, its binding capabilities, and its smoking point. When I'm cooking, I always start with a heated pan before I add the fat. Then the warm fat becomes "home" for the ingredients I am putting together in the dish.

Butter

We use unsalted butter in both our sweet and savory recipes because it allows us to control the amount of salt in a dish. (You can always add more salt if you need to, but you can't take it out.) Butter has a low smoking point, so you need to cook with it carefully. If the milk solids in the butter get too hot, they burn, leaving you with a black and bitter flavor. I like to cook butter over medium heat until it is blond, which is when the butter is completely melted, but the proteins, fat, and water that make it up haven't separated. A gentle browning of butter takes the color one step further. A brown butter will lend a nice, nutty flavor to warm vinaigrettes and soups, bring out the richness of seafood, and balance the sweetness and acidity in vegetable dishes.

Duck Fat

In recent years, it's been easier to come by duck fat at specialty grocery stores; many butcher shops now carry tubs of it as well. Duck fat is lower in saturated fat than other animal fats. Slow cooking duck legs or other animal parts in duck fat until they are fork-tender, a process the French call *confit*, does two things: It gives otherwise tough pieces of meat a place to stay juicy and become tender during the cooking process. And, when you cool the meat in the fat, it offers a great way to preserve it.

Lard

Lard is fat derived from the pig. It mostly comes off the top of the loin and is made from rendering down the fatback with a combination of water and the raw fat. To make lard, you simmer the fatback, which allows the water to eventually evaporate and the melted fat to become the end product. Cooled lard has the same consistency as solid butter and behaves in similar ways. Leaf lard comes from the fat that surrounds the pig's abdomen and is a good substitute for butter in baked goods like shortcrusts and cookies. It's also a great fat for cooking mushrooms and frying chicken and fish. Try to find lard at butcher shops. Supermarkets sometimes sell block lard, but it is processed with chemicals to emulsify and deodorize it. It's not on our recommend list, but works in a pinch.

Suet

Suet is tallow rendered from beef, lamb, sheep, or goat. I get mine from the cows we butcher in-house at The Country Cat and save it for frying chicken. (Suet was the traditional fat used to fry chicken and anything else when commodity fats like Crisco weren't available. Today you can ask your local butcher to source suet for you.) Suet is optimal for frying because it maintains an even temperature throughout the cooking process and has a higher smoking point than other fats. It keeps well and can be reused. When I'm frying chicken in suet, the chicken comes out juicy and full of flavor, and is not greasy at all. When you go through the process of rendering your own suet like you would lard, feel free to throw in bacon scraps or beef or pork trimmings to help flavor the fat. Just avoid adding vegetables, as they have a tendency to burn in the process.

Olive Oil

Olive oil lends acidity, fruitiness, and depth when used in salads and dressings, in the style of *confit* to braise vegetables, and as a finishing agent to drizzle over fish, meats, and vegetables. I use extra-virgin olive oil, as it is the first pressing of the olives and has the best mouthfeel and flavor.

Vegetable Oil

Be it soybean oil, canola oil, or a blend of the two, vegetable oil is light, neutral in flavor, and readily available. I use it primarily to emulsify sauces and dressings when I want the other ingredients, not the flavor of the oil, to shine. Since vegetable oil has a high smoking point, you can also fry foods in it. I say this with great caution, though. Often when you fry something in vegetable oil, your end product will be greasier than it would be if you'd cooked it in animal fat.

Vinegars & Citrus

I tend to have a strong hand with vinegar and citrus and like to keep an assortment in my pantry because different vinegars and citrus fruits provide different levels of acidity and flavor profiles. I always have apple cider vinegar and sherry vinegar in my cupboard. I achieve sweetness and low acidity with apple cider vinegar and use a dash of sherry vinegar when I'm cooking sophisticated, spirited dishes. Freshly squeezed lemon juice and freshly grated lemon zest are the citrus standbys for me. Oranges are a close second. I often reach for a lemon or orange to add a fresh, acidic flavor to salad dressings, soups, cooked greens, or a platter of seafood.

Fresh & Dried Herbs

I use fresh herbs and dried herbs for different purposes in my cooking. I mostly use delicate fresh herbs such as flat-leaf parsley, marjoram, and basil as garnishes or to finish dishes with a fresh hit of flavor at the end of the preparation. I use fresh herbs like rosemary, sage, and thyme in slow-cooking processes and in rubs for meats and fish. These hardier herbs steep into meats and sauces nicely and add more nuanced flavors to a dish.

Dried herbs have become an integral part of my pantry. I have grown to like the flavor they give dredges, dressings, and spice mixes. Their flavors bloom through the cooking and mixing process and remind me of the flavors I grew up eating in the heartland. I especially love the dried herb blend called "herbes de Provence" because it combines rosemary, thyme, savory, oregano, basil, and parsley—all the background herbs I'm looking for in one ingredient. (Some versions contain lavender, but I try to find it without lavender because it can add too much of a perfume-y component to a dish.) If you can't find herbes de Provence, you can easily make your own by combining equal parts of the six dried herbs listed above. Store your dried herbs an airtight container so they will keep their flavor longer, usually around 6 months. If you are having trouble finding a fresh herb, you can substitute a dried one in a recipe by using half as much.

Spices & Seasonings

Spices often come from seeds, peels, roots, stems, and other parts of plants that have been dried. Seasonings are often combinations of spices and herbs together—with the exception of salt.

Salt

Oh, salt. This almighty rock is not only vital to sustaining life, it has been harvested from land and sea to preserve and enhance the flavor of food for thousands of years. Whether I'm using salt to season food, cure meat, or make a brine, most of my recipes call for kosher salt. Jackie also uses kosher salt in sweet dishes to help balance out their sweetness and give them a more well-rounded finish.

I like kosher salt because it is free from impurities and has a cleaner taste than common table salt. When I am looking for a salt to use as a garnish, I reach for a thicker flake sea salt. I use it sparingly, however, as sea salt has a saltier, more intense flavor than kosher salt. Sprinkled over eggs, meats, salads, fish, or even chocolate, a sea salt can bring out and develop flavors.

Spices

Spices add warmth and pop to sauces, dredges, and rubs. When you read through these recipes, you'll see there are certain spices we use more than others. None of them is terribly hard to find. Some of my favorites are lemon pepper, fennel seed, celery seed, and chili flakes. (These are sometimes called red pepper flakes or crushed red pepper.) If a little heat in a recipe isn't your thing, feel free to cut back on the chili flakes or omit them completely.

For the sweet stuff, Jackie always has cinnamon and vanilla handy. She drops cinnamon sticks into compotes and ice cream bases and tosses ground cinnamon into fruit-based desserts to bring added warmth to the palate. Real vanilla extract and whole vanilla beans are good ways to get vanilla flavor into a dish. But if you can find vanilla bean paste at a specialty food store, grab it. It's a great in-between to extract and purchasing pricey vanilla pods. Use it like you would vanilla extract, but expect it to give you a more robust vanilla flavor because the vanilla seeds are present in the paste.

Using freshly ground spices will give dishes a fresher flavor. I try to buy most of my spices whole so I can toast them and grind them as needed. (It also means I'll have whole spices on hand when I need them for brines and marinades.) Whole or ground, I recommend buying spices from stores that sell them in bulk so you can get just the amount you need and use them before they go stale.

Nuts & Seeds

Nuts are a staple item in my cooking. I have to use control with nuts because I want to put them in everything— sides, salads, sautés, you name it. Almonds, pecans, sunflower seeds, cashews, and hazelnuts are among my favorites. Their fat content and crunch make them very versatile ingredients, and they offer texture and a great mouthfeel–especially when they're toasted.

When toasting nuts, spread them out on a large rimmed baking sheet, set your oven to 325°F, and toast them just until they start to turn a pale amber color. (You want to toast nuts low and slow because their natural oils will begin to release as they heat up, increasing the possibility that they'll burn. You can use direct heat from the stovetop to toast nuts but radiant heat from an oven is optimal because stovetop toasting increases the scorching risk.)

I'll use toasted nuts whole or roughly chopped, but I also like to grind them in a blender or food processor to create a nut meal or flour. Nut meals work well as a crust for meat or fish and add an extra dimension to the protein. Buy nuts in smaller quantities to ensure freshness or store them in an airtight container in the freezer for long-term storage so they don't go rancid.

Flours

We use hundreds of pounds of three different flours—all-purpose flour, bread flour, and cake flour—at the restaurant each week to yield different results, depending on what we're cooking. All-purpose flour is just that. We use it for dredges and in most of our baked goods. Bread flour is high in gluten, so when mixed, it produces long, strong strands in the dough that help give bread structure and resilience. Cake flour is low in gluten, which is the protein in wheat-based flours, barley, and rye that provides structure and strength. Jackie blends cake flour and all-purpose flour in our biscuit recipe (page 37) to give the dough just the right amount of structure, while also keeping it light and delicate.

We measure the flour in most of our recipes using dry measuring cups and the scoop-and-sweep method. To measure flour using this method, take your dry measuring cup and scoop it into your flour container. Don't compress the flour by tapping or pressing down on it. Then use the back side of a butter knife and sweep the excess flour off the measuring cup so the flour is level with the rim of the cup. For involved recipes that require more precision, we've measured the flours by weight. The interesting note about measuring flours is that your environment can play a role in how your dough or batter turns out. We find that when it's really dry out, we need to add a little more liquid to a recipe because the flour has less moisture in it, and vice versa when it's humid or rainy.

Chocolate

A simple piece of really good quality chocolate has a creaminess with depth, smoky and toasty nuances that you just don't get with the everyday, humdrum stuff. We have found that if you spend a little extra on better chocolate, your end result will be that much better.

Jackie works mostly with bittersweet chocolate. It's not too sweet and works well in most chocolate-based desserts. Try to find chocolate that is 60 percent cacao for recipes that call for melted chocolate. (We have found that chocolates with higher percentages of cacao tend to break easily when heated. Save those for an afternoon treat.) Be sure to use dry tools when working with chocolate, as it can turn grainy if it comes into contact with water when it is melting.

Unsweetened chocolate—the kind with no added sugar—should not make you pucker with bitterness. Good quality unsweetened chocolate has a robust, deep-toasted cocoa bean taste to it and is a good choice for sweet and savory dishes.

Milk chocolate and semisweet chocolate are best used in cookies and ice creams and to round out deep chocolate dishes like chocolate cakes or tortes.

TECHNIQUES

The craft-driven techniques and methods we share in this book are not terribly hard. Some of them we learned in our training; others we've worked out through trial and error. Take the time and care to learn these techniques and it will pay off when you see your result on the plate.

Grilling

I love cooking with natural heat and have written our grilling recipes with a charcoal barbecue in mind. Natural heat taps all the senses for me and brings an honest, hands-on approach to grilling that teaches you to rely on instinct and learn about smells, touch, heat, intensity, and timing. I keep a selection of charcoal, mesquite, and wood handy, so depending on the item I'm going to grill, I can pick and choose the best heat source. If you only have a gas grill, you can prep it by turning the settings on high and pulling the cover down to raise the heat on the grill grates. When you're ready to start grilling, lift the lid, turn the heat down to medium, and place your item on the grates. By doing this, you will get nice grill marks and help prevent the food from sticking.

Curing

Curing is an age-old way to preserve food and a true art. A dry cure is when a salt-based mixture is liberally rubbed on meat, fish, or certain fruits and vegetables, then weighted and left to sit. A wet cure is when meat, fish, or vegetables are submerged in a salty, sugary liquid called a brine to preserve and season them. Different brands of salts can have different weights, so it's important that you weigh out the salt instead of using volume measurements in our cured meat recipes. (We use Diamond Crystal kosher salt at the restaurant, if you want to do the same.)

Timing is also key when curing an item. The beginning process of a cure is about seasoning the protein or vegetable. With time, the cure penetrates the item and begins to draw moisture out of it. Too much time on the cure, and you can have an overly salty, overcured product. Too little time, and the flavor profile and texture you're trying to achieve won't have a chance to develop. Taking the time to rotate, flip, and turn the item that's on the cure ensures balanced distribution of the cure and process and will show you the various states an item goes through during it. (In the chapters that follow, we've included more detailed descriptions of what to look for during curing steps for individual recipes.)

Smoking

Smoking meats, fish, and vegetables adds a different depth and personality to foods than grilling. Unlike grilling, when you smoke food, you do it slowly at a low temperature. When heated, damp wood smokes, which will then impart deep, soulful character into the food. True wood smoke has a rich flavor, whereas liquid smoke is fake and not worth using. You'll have a blast experimenting with the process and different woods until you find the sweet spot that works for you. I stick with hard woods like alder or hickory. Fruit woods like apple or peach are good, too; just be careful to use them with restraint. The smoke they create can be too thick and tar-laden and can overpower your meat or vegetable.

Smoking Without a Smoker

If you don't have a smoker but do have a charcoal barbecue, you can use it to smoke foods. By making an indirect heat source in a barbecue pit, you are creating the ambient heat needed for smoking as opposed to the direct heat that is used for grilling. While your wood chips are soaking,

build a medium-hot coal fire with charcoal briquettes in your grill and burn the coals to a chalky white. Spread out the coals and move them to one side of the grill, opposite of where you want to place the item. Drain the hickory chips and place them directly onto the coals. Place the item on the grill opposite the coals and hickory chips. Cover the barbecue with the lid and smoke the food according to the recipe instructions, checking on the coals occasionally to make sure the heat stays even.

Braising

Braising is a moist-heat cooking method of extracting and adding flavors through the addition of aromatics, spices, and spirits. This is by far my favorite method for cooking big hunks of pork shoulder, beef chuck, and the meaty but elegant beef short rib. With braising, you get a complete meal that includes fork-tender meat, an amazing sauce with all the integrity of the work you put into it, and vegetables that have soaked up the fruits of your labor.

The dish that epitomizes this technique is the heartland staple, the pot roast. Although the word roast is in the title, it's really all about the braise. Seasoned beef chuck and aromatic vegetables such as carrots, small boiler onions, and potatoes act like sponges for the sauce. A good helping of herbs like rosemary and bay leaf and either chicken stock

or beef stock give the meat and vegetables a home to braise in. I like to get a nice sear on all sides of the meat before adding the vegetables. Then I deglaze the pot with wine and scrape the caramelized meat fond off the bottom to create the flavor base for what's to come. The sear adds depth and color to both the meat and sauce, which is desirable for the final outcome. Combined with time and patience, this will result in success.

Roasting

Roasting is a dry-heat cooking method in which radiant heat penetrates and cooks the meat, fruit, or vegetable from the outside in. The only thing roasting and braising have in common is that the key components of time and patience must come together to produce a full-flavored, well-seasoned, moist, and juicy dish.

For roasting meats in particular, you want a muscle that has a good ratio of marbled fat to lean meat, such as the shoulder from the pig or lamb, a rib-eye from the cow, or a whole chicken, as it's important to have enough fat to aid in the long and slow cooking process.

Roasting gives a deep and intense flavor to the meat by caramelizing the natural sugars and proteins of the animal. Herbs and spices further enhance the natural flavor of the meat. Through roasting, one of the glorious results is a nice crust on the meat. It's my favorite part—I'm guilty of the cardinal sin of picking the crusty, highly seasoned, concentrated meat bits off the top of the roast and enjoying them selfishly because, well, I cooked it!

Depending on the size of the roast, low-and-slow cooking through the afternoon will give you a showpiece roast to feed a family or a gathering of any size. When shopping, I usually purchase 8 ounces of meat per person, which translates to about 6 ounces per serving when it's all said and done, due to moisture loss throughout the cooking process. Before slicing and portioning the roast for the grand finale, let the meat rest for at least 5 minutes. This will help preserve the juices and result in a tender and flavorful cut.

Trussing a roast is an important step in the process of roasting. Often you will get a piece of meat that has had the bone removed, and you will need to put the meat back together using butcher's twine. Holding the meat together this way helps the roast to cook evenly.

TOOLS

To prepare our recipes, you'll need common kitchen tools like baking sheets, a good sharp set of knives, and skillets and saucepans of varying sizes. In addition, the following items are the ones we find useful in the kitchen and nice to have in your pantry.

Baker's Scale
If you don't have a scale in your kitchen, go get one. (A digital scale is ideal, but a standard one works, too.) You will be glad to have one on hand because measuring by weight, especially for curing meats and baking breads, will allow you to get more exact measurements and better results.

Blender
It is always good to have a blender handy to make purees, grind nuts, and blend emulsified dressings. A high-powered tabletop blender with various speed controls will give you enough power to blend, grind, and mix food with ease and precision.

Butcher's Twine
Most grocery and kitchen stores carry spools of the natural white cotton string known as butcher's twine. It is an essential tool for trussing meats, tying together herbs for bouquets garnis, and tying off herb sachets that you'll use to infuse soups and stocks.

Candy Thermometer
When you are cooking sugar on the stovetop to make caramel, a candy thermometer is an important tool to help you see the temperature and learn the stages sugar goes through.

Cast-Iron Skillet
A cast-iron skillet is one of the most affordable, durable, and versatile pans you can buy (see "Cooking with Cast Iron," page 171). Because they

provide such an even source of heat, you can bake in them, sauté in them, and fry in them. (At any given time, we've got four skillets going on our stove at the restaurant.) To keep your pans in prime condition, don't let water sit in them, and scrub them with coarse salt and a green scrubby, not soap, if food sticks to them. (Soap will take the seasoning off along with the food.) If rust forms in the skillet, wipe it out with a dry towel, apply a little bacon fat or oil to the pan, and put it in a 180°F oven to season for a long, slow bake—6 to 8 hours will do.

Charcoal Chimney

If you want an easy, convenient way to start a fire in your grill or barbecue pit, a charcoal chimney is the way to go. You won't even need lighter fluid to get it going. Charcoal chimneys are metal cylinders with a grate inside that allows for airflow. To use one, turn the chimney over and put about three pages of wadded-up newspaper inside it. Jump-start it by lighting the paper, and then flip it over. Fill the chimney with charcoal,

wood, or mesquite. Once the charcoal is ready, dump it into your grill or barbecue pit and get busy.

Deep-Frying Thermometer

A simple deep-frying thermometer helps you to warm frying oil or fat to the right temperature for any given recipe, without risking overheating the oil and burning the food you're frying. Frying temperatures will vary slightly based on the item you are frying, but 350°F is the gold standard for most fried foods.

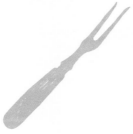

Fish Fork

This is an indispensable tool in my kitchen (see "Where's Gramma?" page 172). A fish fork lends itself to a delicate and exact touch and allows you to move and position food with ease and precision. Other kitchen tools like tongs have a tendency to smash and tear food; a fish fork provides more control and prevents you from overhandling your food.

Hands

Cooking is a craft that should use all your senses, so don't be afraid to get your hands working when you're cooking. Whether you're making

biscuits or forming meatballs, use your hands to get a good feel for the texture of the product. When Jackie makes pie dough or biscuits, I see her using her hands to mix the dough. Once she's turned and folded the dough to help it come together, she rinses her hands and feels the dough again to check if the mix, moisture, and folded layers in the dough are where she wants it. (Touching the dough with cool, rinsed hands refreshes the senses, which enables you to better assess your work.) When I cook meat and vegetables, I use my hands to gauge where the product is in the cooking process. Using your sense of touch helps develop intuition and better understand when something is finished or when it still needs time to cook.

Meat Grinder

When you buy whole animals, as we do at the restaurant, a meat grinder allows you to turn any scrap you get in the butchery process into something useful. In a home kitchen, I recommend using the grinder attachment for a stand mixer because it's more efficient than a hand-crank grinder and comes with all the dies and necessary tools to get you started. If you have the space, store your meat grinder and attachments in the freezer until you're ready to use them. This way they'll be cold enough to prevent the meat from becoming a mushy, creamy mess when you get your meat-grinding and sausage-making projects going.

Microplane™ Grater

I use a fine Microplane grater in almost all of my recipes, usually to get the zest off citrus without removing the pith or for shaving chocolate and hard cheeses. The Microplane shaves citrus zest into a finer flake, which allows it to melt into a dish and provide a citrusy flavor without any hint of acidity.

Parchment Paper

Jackie likes to line baking sheets with parchment paper to prevent the baked goods from sticking or picking up the flavor of the pan. Parchment paper also makes cleanup

much easier when you're roasting a piece of meat. I simply lay a piece of parchment down before I place the roasting rack on the baking sheet. And if you're looking to make a lid for a simmering soup, you can cut parchment paper into a circle of the needed size to fit on top of the pot.

Smoker

If you want to purchase a smoker, I suggest getting a Cookshack™ or The Green Egg™. A Cookshack is an electric smoker that can be set at specific temperatures. It's shaped like a small refrigerator with horizontal shelves and a vertical hinged door. The Green Egg is a nonelectric smoker, so you have to be willing to watch the heat to maintain the temperature you want. It is shaped more like a small ™Weber grill. Both of these smokers work great and are comparable in price, so it really comes down to a matter of preference.

Spice Grinder

I use a coffee grinder to process whole spices such as coriander, fennel seed, or mustard seeds. They are inexpensive and easy to clean, and allow you to have freshly ground spices on hand at all times.

Stand Mixer

You'll use this device way more than you think you will if you don't already have one. A 5- to 6-quart mixer is great for making bread dough, cakes, and cookies. You can also purchase mixer attachments like meat grinders and pasta makers to help make kitchen projects easier. All you have to do is screw the attachment onto the front of your mixer to take your cooking craft to the next level.

AN AMERICAN BREAKFAST

Adam is a gramma at heart. There is no greater satisfaction for him than seeing folks start their day off right with big platters of food. For us, breakfast is a meal where rules are meant to be broken. You can have dessert first by having French toast or pancakes topped with sweetened fruit or a basket of cinnamon rolls before diving into a chicken-fried steak. You can have your eggs poached or over easy, your bacon soft or crisp, and your biscuits fresh out of the oven with honey or jam or fluffy whipped butter. Sweet or savory, hearty or light, a breakfast that fulfills your deepest desires lets you start the day with a meal that fuels body and soul. —JS

Buttermilk Biscuits

Makes 12 to 14 biscuits

In America's heartland, biscuits are practically their own food group. They play an equally important role at the restaurant, where we serve them with gravy, on top of our shellfish potpie, and by the basket with honey or preserves on the side. I worked this recipe years ago by using cake flour to create biscuits with a more delicate crumb. Whether you make them in a stand mixer or by hand, only work the dough until it just comes together. Going past this point can overwork it, leaving you with a stringy, stretchy dough and tough biscuits. By taking an easy hand, you'll get great results every time. —JS

2½ cups (12.5 ounces/356 grams) all-purpose flour, plus more for dusting

1⅔ cups (6.5 ounces/185 grams) cake flour

2 tablespoons baking powder

2 tablespoons sugar

2½ teaspoons kosher salt

½ teaspoon baking soda

1 cup (2 sticks) unsalted butter, cut into ½-inch cubes and chilled, plus more for serving

1¼ cups low-fat buttermilk, chilled

Jam or honey, for serving

1. In the bowl of a stand mixer fitted with the paddle attachment, combine the all-purpose flour, cake flour, baking powder, sugar, salt, and baking soda. Add the butter and mix on low speed until the mixture is the size of peas. With the motor running, add the buttermilk and mix on low speed until the dough just comes together. (You can also whisk the dry ingredients together, cut the butter in by hand, and stir in the buttermilk with a spatula or wooden spoon, if desired.)

2. Turn the dough out onto a clean, lightly floured work surface. Press the dough together so it comes together and form it into a rectangle. Take the far end of the rectangle and fold the dough in half over itself. Press down on the folded mass and give the dough a quarter turn.

Repeat, folding and turning for eight turns. (This process makes layers in the dough that create nice, flaky biscuits as they cook.)

3. Using a lightly floured rolling pin, roll the dough out until it is 1 inch thick and, using a 3-inch biscuit cutter, cut biscuits out of the dough. Line a large baking sheet with parchment paper and transfer the biscuits to the baking sheet, placing them about ½ inch apart. Gather the remaining pieces of dough, reroll to 1 inch thick, and try to get a few more biscuits out of it. Place the biscuits on the baking sheet. Discard any remaining dough.

continued on page 44

4. Cover the biscuits with plastic wrap and place the baking sheet in the freezer for at least 20 minutes or up to 1 week. When the biscuits are chilled, arrange a rack in the center of the oven and preheat the oven to 425°F.

5. Place the biscuits in the oven and bake for 10 minutes. Rotate the baking sheet and decrease the oven temperature to 400°F. Bake the biscuits for 5 minutes more, or until the tops of the biscuits are golden brown and the sides are set but not yet golden brown. Dig in with butter and honey or jam on the side.

1. Working in the butter 2. Pouring in the buttermilk 3. Gently working the dough 4. Prepping the dough to turn out onto the work surface 5. Working the dough into an oblong mass 6. Folding the dough in half 7. Turning the biscuit dough 8. Flattening the dough 9. Cutting the dough in half to see the lovely layers 10. Cutting the biscuits

Ridiculously Good Buttermilk Pancakes

Makes 12 (3-inch) pancakes

I'm a fan of all kinds of pancakes, from gingerbread to hazelnut to pumpkin. But this basic buttermilk variety will always be my favorite. This batter delivers light, fluffy pancakes every time. Here's my secret: I use a stand mixer to combine the ingredients quickly and whip some air into the batter without overmixing it. Serve these pancakes with fresh fruit, a generous pour of pure maple syrup, or a combination of the two. —JS

1½ cups (7.5 ounces/214 grams) all-purpose flour

¼ cup (1.75 ounces/50 grams) sugar

1½ teaspoons baking powder

½ teaspoon baking soda

½ teaspoon kosher salt

1½ cups low-fat buttermilk

2 large eggs

4 tablespoons (½ stick) unsalted butter, melted, plus more for greasing the pan and for serving

¾ teaspoon pure vanilla extract or vanilla bean paste

Nonstick cooking spray (optional)

Fresh fruit and pure maple syrup, for serving

1. In the bowl of a stand mixer fitted with the paddle attachment, combine the flour, sugar, baking powder, baking soda, and salt and mix on low speed until just combined.

2. In a small bowl or glass measuring cup, combine the buttermilk with the eggs and whisk until just combined. Add the buttermilk mixture to the flour mixture and mix on medium speed, scraping down the sides of the bowl with a rubber spatula as needed, until just combined. Add the butter and vanilla and mix on medium-high speed for 10 seconds to beat and smooth the batter. Set the batter aside for 20 minutes to rest at room temperature.

3. Meanwhile, arrange a rack in the center of the oven and preheat the oven to 200°F. In a cast-iron skillet or nonstick skillet set over medium heat, warm a knob of butter until it melts and the foaming subsides. (Alternatively, you can spray the skillet with nonstick cooking spray.) Working in batches, ladle the pancake batter onto the skillet, using about ⅓ cup batter for each pancake and allowing space for the batter to spread a bit. (You don't want the pancakes to touch.) Cook until the bottom of the pancakes are golden brown and the centers are bubbly, about 3 minutes. Using a spatula, flip the pancakes over and cook until the pancakes are set, about 2 minutes more.

4. Transfer the pancakes to a baking sheet and keep warm in the oven while repeating the process with the remaining pancake batter, adding more butter to the skillet as needed. Dig in with butter, fresh fruit, and a drizzle of pure maple syrup on top.

Challah French Toast with Maker's Mark Custard and Clabber Cream

Serves 4

At The Country Cat, we dip thick slabs of homemade Challah Bread (page 50) in a Maker's Mark–spiked custard before they hit the cast-iron skillet. Adding bourbon to the rich custard gives it a flavor boost without being overly boozy. But what really sets this brunch standard apart is what we serve with it: a spoonful of seasonal fruit compote and a generous dollop of clabber cream.

Clabber cream is an old-fashioned spooning cream that we make using heavy cream, confectioners' sugar, and sour cream. It's got a great tang that offsets the sweetness of the French toast—just think of it as America's answer to that French favorite, crème fraîche. —JS

Clabber Cream

½ cup heavy cream

½ cup (2 ounces/56 grams) confectioners' sugar

1 cup full-fat sour cream

1½ teaspoons pure vanilla extract or vanilla bean paste

Finely grated zest of ½ orange

Challah French Toast

8 large eggs

2 cups half-and-half

3 tablespoons bourbon, preferably Maker's Mark

2 tablespoons pure vanilla extract or vanilla bean paste

2 tablespoons ground cinnamon

1 large loaf homemade Challah Bread (page 50) or store-bought

3 tablespoons unsalted butter

Dried Fruit Compote (page 281), for garnish (optional)

Confectioners' sugar, for garnish

Nonstick cooking spray (optional)

continued on page 48

1. **Make the clabber cream:** In the bowl of a stand mixer fitted with the whisk attachment, combine the cream with the confectioners' sugar and whisk on medium speed until medium peaks form. Using a rubber spatula, fold in the sour cream, vanilla, and orange zest until combined. Refrigerate the clabber cream until ready to use.

2. **Make the challah French toast:** Arrange a rack in the center of the oven and preheat the oven to 200°F. Warm a 12-inch cast-iron skillet over low heat.

3. Meanwhile, in a large bowl, combine the eggs, half-and-half, bourbon, vanilla, and cinnamon and whisk until combined. Set aside. Slice the challah crosswise on an angle into eight ½-inch-thick slices and set aside. (Reserve any remaining challah for another use.)

4. Raise the heat under the skillet to medium. When the skillet is hot, warm a knob of butter in the skillet until it melts and the foaming subsides. (Alternatively, you can spray the skillet with nonstick cooking spray.)

5. Working in batches, dip the challah slices in the custard mixture, pressing the bread down into the custard so it soaks up a good amount. Place the slices in the skillet and cook until golden brown on each side, about 3 minutes per side. Transfer the slices to a large baking sheet and keep warm in the oven while repeating the process with the remaining slices, adding more butter to the skillet as needed.

6. Remove the baking sheet from the oven and divide the slices among four plates. Garnish each serving with a generous spoonful of the clabber cream and dried fruit compote (if using). Dust the entire dish with confectioners' sugar and dig in.

Challah Bread

Makes 2 large loaves

Everyone should make challah at least once in their lifetime. It is a gorgeous bread to look at, with its braided design, and as satisfying to make as it is to eat. My longtime pastry assistant, Leah Miller, inspired this recipe. We make a six-braid loaf instead of the more conventional three-braid loaf because it's all the more impressive. Whenever we're braiding the dough, the cooks crowd around to watch the rhythmic process. As I work, I chant quietly to myself so I don't forget the braiding pattern, "Second crosses over; first divides the rest. Second crosses over; first divides the rest." When the loaf comes out of the oven, you'll agree that there is something magical about it.

Use this bread to make killer Challah French Toast (page 47) or just serve thick slices with butter, jam, or honey. —JS

1 tablespoon active dry yeast

¼ cup (1.75 ounces/50 grams) sugar

4 large eggs

½ cup vegetable oil

2 tablespoons honey

5⅓ cups (1 pound 11 ounces/768 grams) all-purpose flour, plus more as needed

2 teaspoons kosher salt

Nonstick cooking spray

1 egg yolk

1. Place 1 cup warm water (about 110°F) in the bowl of a stand mixer and sprinkle the yeast over the top. Whisk to combine. Add the sugar and whisk to combine. Let the mixture rest at room temperature until the yeast dissolves, about 4 minutes.

2. Add the whole eggs, oil, and honey to the bowl and stir to combine. Add the flour and the salt. Using the dough hook attachment, mix the dough on low speed for 1 minute to incorporate the ingredients. Raise the speed to medium and mix the dough until it is smooth and elastic, about 10 minutes. (The dough should not be overly wet, but will be slightly sticky. If the dough seems too wet, sprinkle a little additional flour into the bowl and mix for a few minutes longer.)

3. Grease a large bowl with nonstick cooking spray. Turn the dough into the bowl and cover with plastic wrap. Let the dough rest in a warm place until nearly doubled, about 1 hour 20 minutes.

4. Punch down the dough and divide it into two equal balls. Cover one ball with plastic wrap or a damp kitchen towel and set aside. Divide the other ball into six equal pieces. Working with one piece at a time on a clean work surface, roll the pieces into 16-inch ropes that are about the thickness of your thumb. (You can lightly flour your hands if you find the dough is too sticky to work with.)

5. Pinch the ropes together at the top and begin the braiding process. (See the illustrations on the following pages.) Starting from the left side, take the second rope and cross it all the way over to the right so it overlaps and lays horizontally across the other ropes. Take what was the first rope on the right and overlap it so it will come down in between the third and the fourth rope. Now, starting from the right side, take the second rope and cross it over the other ropes to the left. Take what was the first rope from the left and cross it to divide between the third rope. Start the process again, starting from the left. Continue braiding, alternating each side until the entire loaf is braided. Once you are at the bottom of the loaf, pinch the ends together and fold them underneath the loaf so the end looks nice and neat.

6. Line a baking sheet with parchment paper and grease the paper as well. Transfer the braided loaf to the prepared baking sheet and cover it with a damp kitchen towel while you roll out the remaining ball and braid the ropes to form the second loaf. Transfer the second loaf to the prepared baking sheet. Cover the loaves with plastic wrap and let them rest in a warm place until nearly doubled in size, about 1 hour.

7. When the loaves are ready, arrange a rack in the center of the oven and preheat the oven to 375°F. In a small bowl, combine the egg yolk with 2 tablespoons water and whisk to combine. Using a pastry brush, brush the loaves evenly with the egg wash. Bake the loaves for 25 to 35 minutes or until they are golden brown and sound hollow when you tap them.

8. Remove the loaves from the oven and let cool completely on the baking sheet before slicing. Wrapped tightly in plastic wrap, the loaves will keep at room temperature for 3 days or in the freezer for up to 1 month.

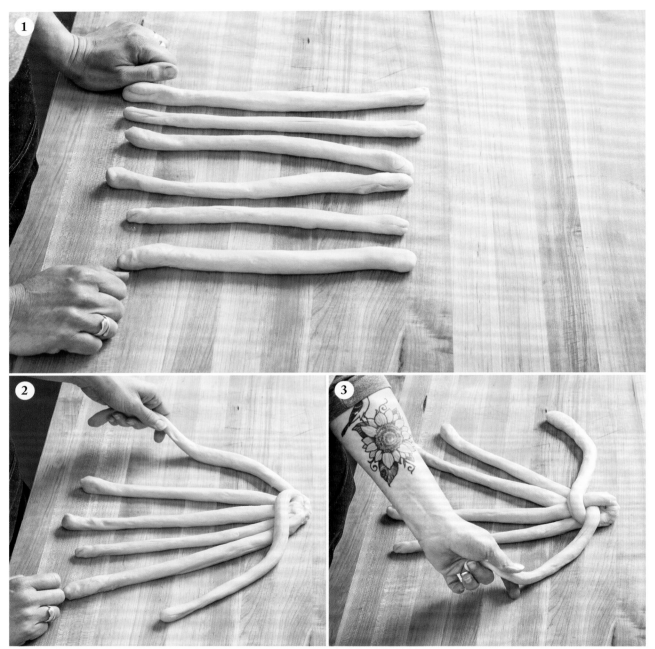

1. Rolling the ropes 2. Starting the braid 3. Getting into the braid 4. Working through the braid 5. Finishing the braid 6. Brushing the braid with an egg wash

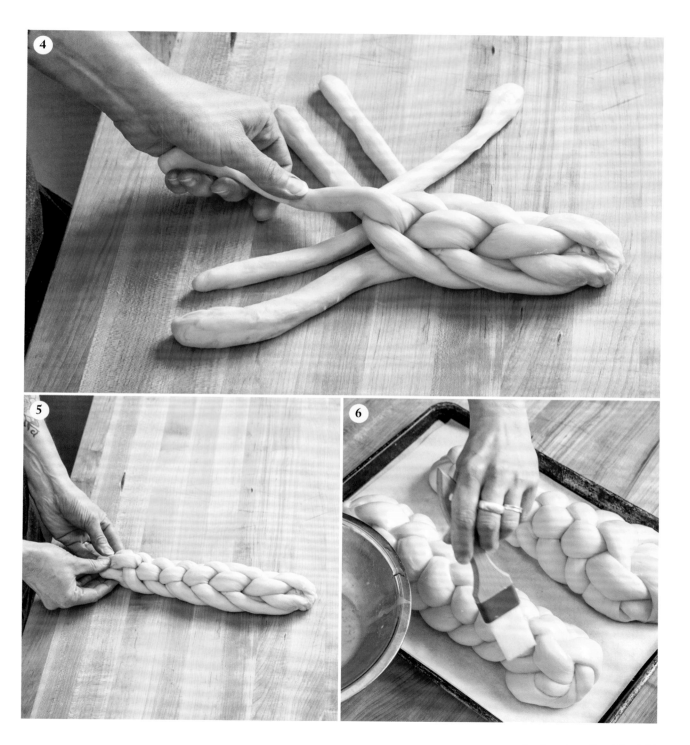

Brioche Pecan Cinnamon Rolls

Makes 15 cinnamon rolls

I go the extra mile with my cinnamon rolls by making them from brioche dough, which has a better depth of flavor than a regular yeasted dough. Brioche can be tricky to make. I've found I have more success when I measure the bread flour by weight, not volume. (You'll need a kitchen scale for this step.) Some people like to bring brioche dough up to room temperature before rolling it out, but I like to work with the sticky dough when it's cold because it's easier to deal with, especially when you are slicing the log into rolls. If pecans aren't your thing, you can leave them out, substitute a different nut, or use raisins in the intensely cinnamon-y filling. —JS

Brioche Dough

¾ cup whole milk

1½ teaspoons active dry yeast

3¾ cups (1¼ pounds/567 grams) bread flour, plus more for dusting

1¾ teaspoons granulated sugar

1½ teaspoons kosher salt

3 large eggs

1 egg yolk

¾ cup (1½ sticks) unsalted butter, at room temperature

Nonstick cooking spray

Pecan Filling

1 cup (2 sticks) unsalted butter, at room temperature

1 cup (7.5 ounces/214 grams) packed light brown sugar

3 tablespoons ground cinnamon

1 tablespoon pure vanilla extract or vanilla bean paste

1 teaspoon kosher salt

1 cup roughly chopped pecans, toasted (see Chef's Note)

Brown Sugar Glaze

1 cup (4 ounces/112 grams) confectioners' sugar

8 tablespoons (1 stick) unsalted butter, cut into ½-inch cubes

¼ cup (2 ounces/57 grams) packed light brown sugar

2 tablespoons whole milk

2 teaspoons ground cinnamon

½ teaspoon pure vanilla extract or vanilla bean paste

1. **Make the brioche dough:** The day before baking the cinnamon rolls, in a small saucepan, gently warm the milk over medium-low heat until lukewarm or until it reaches 110°F on a digital thermometer.

2. In the bowl of a stand mixer, combine the milk with the yeast and whisk to combine. Let the mixture rest at room temperature until the yeast has dissolved, about 10 minutes. Meanwhile, in a large bowl, combine the flour granulated sugar, and salt and whisk to combine. Set aside.

3. In a small bowl or glass measuring cup, combine the whole eggs with the egg yolk and whisk to combine. Add the eggs, then the flour mixture to the milk mixture in the stand mixer bowl. Fit the stand mixer with the dough hook and mix on low speed, scraping the sides of the bowl with a rubber spatula as needed, until just combined. With the motor running, gradually add the butter, 1 tablespoon at a time. Once all the butter has been incorporated, mix the dough until it is smooth and elastic, about 8 minutes. Turn the dough out onto a clean work surface and knead until the dough is smooth in appearance, about 5 minutes.

4. Grease a large bowl with nonstick cooking spray. Transfer the dough to the bowl and cover it with plastic wrap. Let the dough rest in a warm place until doubled in size, about 2 hours 30 minutes. Punch down the dough, cover the bowl with plastic wrap, and let it rest in the refrigerator overnight.

5. **Make the pecan filling:** The next day, in the bowl of a stand mixer fitted with the paddle attachment, combine the butter, brown sugar, cinnamon, vanilla, and salt and mix on medium speed until light and fluffy, about 3 minutes. Add the pecans and mix until just combined. Set aside.

6. Turn the dough out onto a clean, lightly floured work surface and shape it into a rectangle. Roll out the dough until it is about 12 by 18 inches and ¼ inch thick, while maintaining the rectangular shape as much as possible. Using a spatula, spread the filling uniformly over the dough. (The filling will be fairly thick.)

7. With the long side of the dough facing you, take the edge of the dough closest to you and gently roll the dough away from you. (You want this initial fold to be tight so you get a nice spiral in the center of the cinnamon roll.) Run your hands along the dough so your roll is uniform and even, then continue rolling the dough until you've reached the end. With the seam facing down and using a sharp serrated knife, cut the log crosswise into 1-inch-thick cinnamon rolls.

8. Coat a 9 by 13-inch baking pan with nonstick cooking spray. Arrange the cinnamon rolls snugly in the pan, cover the pan with plastic wrap, and let the cinnamon rolls rest at room temperature for 30 minutes.

9. Meanwhile, arrange a rack in the center of the oven and preheat the oven to 350°F. Uncover the cinnamon rolls and bake for 30 minutes or until golden brown but still soft. Remove the cinnamon rolls from the oven and let them rest while making the glaze.

10. **Make the brown sugar glaze:** In a small saucepan, combine the confectioners' sugar, butter, brown sugar, milk, cinnamon, and vanilla. Cook over medium heat, whisking frequently, until the butter has melted and the glaze looks thick and shiny, about 5 minutes. Spoon the glaze generously over the rolls and dig in.

Chef's Note: To toast nuts such as pecans or walnuts, arrange a rack in the center of the oven and preheat the oven to 325°F. Spread the nuts evenly on a baking sheet and bake for 20 minutes or until they are toasty and golden brown.

Brioche Pecan Cinnamon Rolls, page 54

Slow Burn, page 58

Slow Burn

Serves 4 to 6

This stick-to-your-ribs chili is perfect for any weekend day spent lounging around watching football games. We use this particular mix of chiles to give the dish plenty of toasty, smoky flavors, and we throw in a little chocolate to give the chili added depth. You're getting yourself into a more involved cooking process when you make this recipe, but you'll find that the sofrito and chile puree are easy to make and key to building complex flavors. (If you like, you can make everything ahead of time and throw the chili in a slow cooker to keep it warm.) Our sous chef Mike Eells came up with this recipe to serve with sunny-side-up eggs and grits, and we recommend doing the same no matter what time of day you serve it. The grits help balance out the heat in the chili, and the eggs just push it over the top.

If you don't have access to a smoker, you can still make an excellent version of this dish by omitting step 2. In step 1, let the pork rest for one hour at room temperature or covered and refrigerated for up to twenty-four hours to let the rub penetrate the meat before proceeding with the recipe. —AS

Pork Shoulder

2½ tablespoons packed light brown sugar

2½ tablespoons kosher salt

1½ teaspoons sweet paprika

1 teaspoon ground cumin

1 teaspoon dried oregano

½ teaspoon cayenne pepper

2½ pounds boneless pork shoulder, cut into 6 equal pieces

¼ cup vegetable oil

1 medium yellow onion, thinly sliced

½ cup chicken stock

1¼ ounces unsweetened chocolate

3 teaspoons granulated sugar

3 teaspoons distilled white vinegar

Sofrito

1 (14.5-ounce) can whole peeled tomatoes

⅔ cup fresh cilantro leaves, roughly chopped

½ medium yellow onion, diced

2 garlic cloves, finely chopped

1 tablespoon freshly squeezed lime juice

1 teaspoon chili flakes

Chile Puree

2 dried ancho chiles

2 dried cascabel chiles

2 dried pasilla chiles

1 chipotle pepper in adobo sauce

1. **Make the pork shoulder:** In a large bowl, combine the brown sugar, salt, paprika, cumin, oregano, and cayenne and whisk to combine. Add the pork shoulder and mix to coat the pork shoulder evenly with the spice mixture. Set aside.

2. Soak the wood chips according to package instructions and preheat a smoker to 225°F. (Or see "Smoking Without a Smoker," page 35.) Place the wet hickory chips over the fire or in an electric hopper and smoke the pork for 1 hour.

3. **Meanwhile, make the sofrito:** In the bowl of a food processor fitted with the steel blade, combine the tomatoes, cilantro, onion, garlic, lime juice, and chili flakes and puree until smooth. Transfer the mixture to a small bowl and set aside.

4. **Make the chile puree:** In a medium saucepan, combine the ancho chiles, cascabel chiles, and pasilla chiles and add water to cover. Cover the saucepan and bring to a simmer over medium heat. Cook the chiles until tender, about 15 minutes. Drain the chiles and transfer to a cutting board to cool slightly. Using a sharp knife, remove the stems, veins, and seeds.

5. In the bowl of a food processor fitted with the steel blade, combine the chiles and chipotle pepper and puree until smooth. Add the chile mixture to the sofrito and set aside.

6. When the pork is ready, arrange a rack in the center of the oven and preheat the oven to 350°F.

7. Meanwhile, in a large Dutch oven set over medium heat, warm the oil. Add the pork and cook until browned on all sides, about 5 minutes per side. Transfer the pork to a plate and set aside.

8. Reduce the heat to medium-low, add the onion to the pot, and cook, stirring occasionally, until translucent, about 5 minutes. Add the stock, using a wooden spoon or spatula to scrape up the brown bits from the bottom of the pot. Add the sofrito-chile mixture to the pot and bring the mixture to a gentle simmer. Add the chocolate, granulated sugar, and vinegar and stir to combine. Cook until the chocolate has melted, about 5 minutes.

9. Bury the reserved pork in the chile base, cover, and cook for 2 hours 30 minutes to 3 hours, or until you can easily shred the pork with two forks. Remove the pot from the oven and let the pork sit, covered, for 30 minutes.

10. Using a whisk, break the meat into shreds to form a chunky, hearty chili. Divide the chili among four to six bowls and dig in.

Morel and Spring Vegetable Hash

Serves 4 to 6

This hearty vegetarian hash kicks off spring by combining English peas, baby spinach, morels, and spring onions with crispy potatoes. Farmers harvest mild spring onions before the bulbs grow to full size; they have small white or deep purple bulbs and tall green tops. (Use two sweet onions if you can't find spring onions.) Morels are my favorite mushroom to use in this hash, but you can also substitute your favorite mushroom if you don't want to splurge on morels. Serve the hash on its own or dish it up with poached eggs and toast to make it a more substantial meal. —AS

4 large red potatoes, cut into ½-inch pieces

¼ cup extra-virgin olive oil

1 tablespoon finely chopped fresh rosemary

Kosher salt and freshly ground black pepper

½ pound fresh morel mushrooms

2 tablespoons unsalted butter

½ pound asparagus, trimmed and cut into 1-inch pieces

4 spring onions, trimmed and cut into ¼-inch rings

2 garlic cloves, finely chopped

2 tablespoons finely chopped fresh flat-leaf parsley

2 tablespoons finely chopped fresh thyme

Finely grated zest and freshly squeezed juice of ½ lemon

½ pound fresh or frozen shelled English peas

4 cups tightly packed baby spinach

1. Arrange a rack in the center of the oven and preheat the oven to 400°F.

2. In a medium bowl, toss the potatoes with the oil, rosemary, and a pinch of salt and pepper. Transfer the potatoes to a large baking sheet and roast for 30 minutes or until crispy and fork-tender. Remove the potatoes from the oven and set aside.

3. Bring a medium pot of salted water to a boil. Add the morels and boil for 10 seconds. (This cleans the morels and kills any worms or spores that might be in them.) Using a slotted spoon, transfer the morels to a cutting board. Pat the morels dry, halve them, and set aside.

4. In a 12-inch cast-iron skillet set over medium heat, melt the butter and cook until blond. Add the asparagus and spring onions and cook, stirring occasionally, until the onions start to wilt and the asparagus gets a little color on it, about 3 minutes. Add the garlic and cook, stirring occasionally, until golden brown, about 1 minute. Add the morels, cover the skillet, and cook until the morels release their natural juices, about 1 minute.

5. Remove the lid from the skillet and add the potatoes, parsley, thyme, lemon zest, and lemon juice and stir to combine. Add the peas and spinach, stir to combine, and cook, stirring frequently, until the spinach wilts, about 2 minutes. Season with salt and pepper.

6. Using a large serving spoon, divide the hash among four to six large bowls or plates. Now eat.

My Smoky Bacon

Makes 4½ to 5 pounds

When someone asks me to teach them how to cure meats, I always start with bacon. The recipe is very forgiving, promises quick results, and only requires minimal hands-on time once you've assembled the ingredients and made the cure for the pork belly. (Just make sure you weigh the sugar and salt using a kitchen scale, not volume measurements, to ensure accuracy.) After you've smoked the pork belly, you can use the bacon in collard greens, hashes, and vinaigrettes or serve it solo as a sweet-salty side dish.

A note about the ingredients: You can preorder a large pork belly through a local butcher or farmers' market vendors, and you can find the curing salt at a specialty store like The Meadow, which has locations in Portland and New York City as well as an online shop. The curing salt I use is called Prague Powder No. 1 and has a slightly pink tint. —AS

4 ounces packed light brown sugar

4 ounces kosher salt

¾ ounce granulated sugar

2 tablespoons roughly chopped fresh flat-leaf parsley

2 tablespoons roughly chopped fresh sage leaves

2 tablespoons roughly chopped fresh thyme

2 teaspoons freshly ground black pepper

1 teaspoon cayenne pepper

1 teaspoon ground coriander

1 teaspoon curing salt

1 teaspoon ground ginger

1 teaspoon ground juniper berries

1 (5-pound) pork belly

2 cups hickory chips, for smoking

1. In a large bowl, combine the brown sugar, kosher salt, granulated sugar, parsley, sage, thyme, pepper, cayenne, coriander, curing salt, ginger, and juniper berries and whisk until combined. (You should have slightly more than 1½ cups cure.) On a clean work surface, season the pork belly liberally on all sides with the cure.

2. Transfer the pork belly to a large glass or nonreactive baking pan. Cover the pan with plastic wrap. Place a large baking sheet on top of the pork belly and weigh it down with a few heavy cans. (The larger the cans, the better; even dumbbells work. Your goal is to have about 30 pounds of weight resting on top of the pork belly, so be sure to put it on the bottom shelf of your refrigerator.) Refrigerate the pork belly for 3 days.

3. After 3 days of curing, flip the pork belly over, cover it with plastic wrap, and place the baking sheet and weights on top of it again. Refrigerate the pork belly until firm to the touch, about 4 days more.

4. Remove the pork belly from the refrigerator and let it come to room temperature. Meanwhile, soak the hickory chips according to package instructions and preheat a smoker to 225°F. Place the wet hickory chips over the fire or in an electric hopper and smoke the pork belly for 2 hours 30 minutes, according to the manufacturer's instructions. (Do not worry about turning the pork belly–just let it roll.)

5. When the bacon is finished smoking, transfer it to a large pan and refrigerate it overnight. Slice the bacon as desired and store in the refrigerator in an airtight container for up to 2 weeks.

Breakfast Sausage with Maple Mustard

Makes 4½ pounds

When sausage hits the breakfast table, I know it isn't going to be an ordinary meal—especially when the sausage is homemade. This breakfast sausage is for DIY enthusiasts who want to try their hand at making an easy sausage that they can store in the freezer and pull out when needed. To keep the pork shoulder in good shape, it's crucial that you keep it cold so that you don't have a meaty mess on your hands when you grind it.

Because charcuterie recipes like this sausage require precision, you will need a kitchen scale for weighing out the seasonings. To grind the pork shoulder, I recommend using a stand mixer with a meat grinder attachment, though you can use a hand-cranked grinder, too. Keep all of the grinder parts in the freezer so everything is as cold as possible when you are ready to grind the meat. Then you can shape the sausage into patties or, if you have a stuffer, get pork casings from your local butcher store and stuff away. —AS

2 ounces light brown sugar

1½ ounces kosher salt, plus more for seasoning

½ ounce ground coriander

½ ounce dried thyme

½ ounce ground fennel seed

¼ ounce ground celery seed

¼ ounce garlic powder

¼ ounce freshly ground black pepper, plus more for seasoning

4½ pounds boneless pork shoulder, cut into 1-inch cubes

Vegetable oil, for cooking

Maple Mustard (opposite), for serving

1. In a medium bowl, combine the sugar, salt, coriander, thyme, fennel seed, celery seed, garlic powder, and pepper.

2. Place the pork shoulder in a large bowl and sprinkle one-third of the sugar-spice mixture over the top. Using your hands, mix thoroughly to combine. Repeat the sprinkling and mixing process until all of the sugar-spice mixture is mixed into the pork shoulder. Cover the bowl with plastic wrap and place the pork shoulder in the freezer until nearly frozen, about 2 hours.

3. When the pork shoulder is chilled, fill a large bowl with ice and water and place a second large bowl in the ice water. Place the bowls under the output of the meat grinder. Grind the pork shoulder through the small die of the meat grinder into the chilled bowl.

4. Portion a small patty out of the ground pork. In a large skillet set over medium-high heat, cook the patty until the edges are lightly caramelized, flipping it halfway through. Taste the patty and adjust the seasoning with additional salt and pepper.

5. Portion out the sausage into 3-ounce patties. (You should have about 24 patties; they'll be about the size of hockey pucks.) Transfer the patties to an airtight container and refrigerate for up to 3 days or freeze for up to 1 month. To cook the sausage, in a large skillet set over medium-high heat, warm 1 tablespoon of vegetable oil. Cook the patties until crispy and golden brown, flipping them halfway through, about 4 minutes per side. Dig in, serving a dollop of maple mustard on the side.

Maple Mustard

Makes 1 cup

This sweet-savory condiment bridges the gap between breakfast and lunch. We like to serve it with our breakfast sausage for brunch, but you could also use it to glaze a pork loin or put it on a ham sandwich. —AS

1 cup good quality whole-grain mustard

2 tablespoons pure maple syrup

In a small bowl, combine the mustard and maple syrup and whisk to combine. Use immediately or store in an airtight container in the refrigerator for up to 2 weeks.

THE GOOD EGG

Making eggs can really test a cook's patience. If you don't use proper technique, a lot can go wrong in the pan. The eggs can break. They can brown too quickly and taste bitter. The yolks can get overcooked. The whites might not set. For such a simple food, eggs are deceptively challenging to cook.

We go through more than six thousand eggs a week at The Country Cat and, over time, have come up with a toolbox of tips and tricks to cook eggs properly. For me, it starts with the pan. Even if you don't use nonstick pans regularly, it pays to keep one on hand for frying, flipping, and scrambling eggs with ease and control. When it comes to poaching, it's all about the saucepan. I fill a medium saucepan three-quarters full with water and bring it to a simmer. Then I add enough white distilled vinegar so you can really taste it in the water, which ends up being about ¼ cup. (The vinegar helps set and stabilize the egg white.) When the water boils, I swirl the water, then crack the egg into it so the white spins and encapsulates the yolk. The whole effect is kind of like a tornado, and the poached eggs come out looking like perfect white orbs.

Heat is an important consideration, too. The temperature you use to cook eggs will make or break (no pun intended) your finished product. To make scrambled eggs that are sweet, luscious, supple, and pale yellow, use low to medium heat and stir the eggs continuously. For fried eggs, start the heat at medium-low, then raise the heat to medium-high and cook the eggs until the whites release easily from the pan. After flipping the eggs, turn off the heat and let the residual heat finish cooking the yolks. We go about 30 seconds for over-easy eggs and increase the resting time in 30-second increments for medium eggs all the way up to a hard, fully set yolk.

When it comes to fats, I'm a fan of cooking my everyday breakfast eggs in butter or bacon fat because those fats render a sweeter-tasting egg. My mom cooked eggs for me this way throughout my childhood and served them up with bacon and buttered toast on the side. If I cook eggs in olive oil, I'm after a more savory, Mediterranean-style egg that I can eat on top of a big piece of crusty salty bread with lots of black pepper. Add a Bloody Mary to the mix, and my morning is just about perfect.

Finally, eggs need salt—especially the whites. A thick flake sea salt like Jacobsen Salt Co.'s sea salt from Netarts Bay, Oregon, is ideal. I also garnish my eggs with coarsely ground black pepper right from the pepper mill. More than anything, the seasoning is what brings an egg to life. —AS

THE GARDEN

Nothing shows off the season better than a carefully composed salad. When it comes to selecting the ingredients, I like to pair delicate vegetables with a masculine component like crispy fried pig's ears, or match a juicy summer fruit like melon with savory herbs and greens to create unexpected salads with a range of textures and flavors. A simple vinaigrette or a cream-based dressing like ranch that ties these ingredients together and offers a perfect balance of fat and acid is the final step in creating a harmonious experience on the plate. —AS

Wedge Salad with Soft Poached Egg and Green Goddess Dressing

Serves 6 (makes about 2½ cups dressing)

The wedge salad is an American classic and steakhouse staple. I've updated the dish by dressing it with an herby green goddess dressing and by adding a poached egg to make the salad more substantial. Make sure you serve this salad with steak knives so guests can easily cut through the wedge.

You should also know that this recipe makes a ton of dressing. You'll want to hang on to the leftovers because it only gets better with time. And it makes a great dipping sauce for our Skillet-Fried Chicken (page 156), "Sappy Spice" Grilled Chicken (page 159), and home fries (see Chef's Note, page 231). —AS

Green Goddess Dressing

2 large egg yolks

2 garlic cloves

2 tablespoons freshly squeezed orange juice

1½ tablespoons freshly squeezed lemon juice, plus more for seasoning

1½ tablespoons freshly squeezed lime juice

2 cups vegetable oil

1 cup loosely packed fresh flat-leaf parsley

2 tablespoons fresh tarragon

¼ medium avocado, roughly chopped

Kosher salt

2 tablespoons heavy cream

Wedge Salad and Soft Poached Egg

3 tablespoons distilled white vinegar

6 large eggs

3 medium heads butter lettuce, halved

Kosher salt and freshly ground black pepper

1 tablespoon finely chopped fresh flat-leaf parsley

Extra-virgin olive oil, for garnish

continued on page 72

1. **Make the green goddess dressing:** In a blender or in the bowl of a food processor fitted with the steel blade, combine the egg yolks, garlic, orange juice, lemon juice, and lime juice and blend on low speed or process until smooth. With the motor running, slowly add 1 cup of the oil to create an emulsion. Raise the speed to medium-high, add the parsley and tarragon, and blend until combined. With the motor running, slowly add the remaining 1 cup oil to complete the emulsion. Add the avocado and blend until smooth. Season with salt and additional lemon juice, if needed.

2. Transfer the dressing to a medium bowl and slowly whisk in the cream. (The dressing should be thick enough to coat the back of a spoon.) Set the dressing aside.

3. **Make the wedge salad and soft poached egg:** In a medium saucepan , combine the vinegar with 4 cups water and bring to a gentle simmer over medium heat. When the water boils, swirl the water, gently crack the eggs into the simmering water and cook until the whites are set but the yolks are still runny, about 3 minutes.

4. While the eggs are poaching, spoon 2 tablespoons of the dressing onto each of six plates and place a lettuce wedge cut-side up on top of the dressing. Spoon an additional 1 tablespoon of the dressing on top of the lettuce on each plate. (Reserve the remaining dressing for another use. Stored in an airtight container in the refrigerator, the dressing will keep for up to 5 days.)

5. Using a slotted spoon, carefully remove the eggs from the saucepan and place one on top of each lettuce wedge. Sprinkle a little salt and parsley over the egg. Lightly drizzle the salad with olive oil on top of each egg.

Chanterelle, Green Bean, and Freekeh Salad with Huckleberry Vinaigrette

Serves 4 (makes about 2 cups vinaigrette)

I discovered freekeh during a time in my cooking career when I was searching for new grains to work with. I love the roasted green wheat's earthy, smoky flavor and ability to act like farro in a grain salad or like rice in risotto-type dishes. Here, I serve the toothsome grain in a late-summer salad with green beans and chanterelles cooked in brandy and butter. The full-flavored huckleberry vinaigrette ties everything together with a hint of sweetness. (You can substitute blueberries if you can't find huckleberries.) You will have leftover vinaigrette; use it to punch up everyday green salads or spoon it over grilled chicken or pork. —AS

Huckleberry Vinaigrette

1 pint (2 cups) fresh huckleberries

⅓ cup balsamic vinegar

1 tablespoon finely chopped fresh thyme

2 small shallots, finely chopped

½ cup extra-virgin olive oil

Kosher salt and freshly ground black pepper

Chanterelle, Green Bean, and Freekeh Salad

1 cup freekeh

Kosher salt

½ pound small chanterelle mushrooms

2 tablespoons unsalted butter

½ cup brandy

1 tablespoon finely chopped fresh thyme

¾ pound green beans, trimmed and halved

continued on page 75

1. **Make the huckleberry vinaigrette:** In a blender or the bowl of a food processor fitted with the steel blade, puree ¼ cup of the huckleberries. (You should have about 3 tablespoons puree.) In a small bowl or large glass measuring cup, combine the puree with the vinegar, thyme, and shallots. Whisk to combine while slowly pouring in the oil. Season with salt and pepper. Gently stir the remaining 1¾ cups huckleberries into the vinaigrette and set aside.

2. **Make the chanterelle, green bean, and freekeh salad:** In a medium saucepan, combine the freekeh with 4 cups salted water and bring to a boil over medium-high heat. Reduce the heat to medium-low and simmer until the freekeh is tender but still has some bite to it, about 12 minutes. Drain the freekeh, cover to keep warm, and set aside.

3. Meanwhile, using a pastry brush, gently clean any dirt off the chanterelles. In a large skillet set over medium heat, warm the butter until it melts. Add the chanterelles and a pinch of salt and, once they start sizzling, add the brandy and thyme. Cook, stirring occasionally, until the chanterelles are firm and meaty and all the liquid has evaporated, 10 to 20 minutes. (If you are using early season chanterelles in July, cook them for 20 minutes. If you are using late season chanterelles in the fall, cook them for 10 minutes.) Remove the skillet from the heat, cover to keep warm, and set aside.

4. While the chanterelles are cooking, fill a large bowl with ice and water, salt the water, and set aside. Bring a medium pot of salted water to a boil. Add the green beans and cook until just tender, about 3 minutes. Transfer the beans to the ice water bath and chill until cold. Drain and set aside.

5. Spoon about ½ cup of freekeh onto each of four plates. In a medium bowl, toss the green beans with some of the vinaigrette. Arrange the green beans in haystack-like piles on top of the freekeh. Then divide the chanterelles among the four plates. Drizzle additional vinaigrette around the plate. (Reserve any remaining vinaigrette for another use. Stored in an airtight container in the refrigerator, it will keep for up to 4 days.) Dig in.

Grilled Corn Salad with Bing Cherries and Goat Cheese

Serves 4

When corn and Bing cherries hit the market each summer, I like to combine them in this colorful corn salad. Plump Bing cherries add a great, almost meaty texture to the dish and, because they aren't overly sweet, provide a perfect contrast to the natural sweetness of fresh summer corn. Serve this salad as a starter or on the side of "Sappy Spice" Grilled Chicken (page 159) for a light summer meal. —AS

4 large ears corn

1 small shallot, finely chopped

¼ cup apple cider vinegar

¾ cup extra-virgin olive oil

Kosher salt and freshly ground black pepper

½ medium fennel bulb, thinly sliced

½ pound Bing cherries, pitted and halved

2 tablespoons finely chopped fresh flat-leaf parsley

1 tablespoon finely chopped fresh marjoram

1 tablespoon finely chopped fresh thyme

2 cups packed mizuna

2 ounces fresh goat cheese

1. Prepare a hot fire in a charcoal grill. Meanwhile, remove all but the innermost layer of husk from each ear of corn and set the ears of corn aside. When the grill is hot, place the corn over direct heat. Grill the corn, turning occasionally, until the husks begin to blacken, about 7 minutes. Remove the corn from the grill and set aside to cool.

2. In a medium bowl, combine the shallot with the vinegar. Add the oil and whisk to combine. Season with salt and pepper. Set aside.

3. Husk the grilled corn and cut the kernels off the cobs. Add the corn kernels to the bowl with the vinaigrette and add the fennel, cherries, parsley, marjoram, and thyme and stir to combine.

4. Divide the mizuna among four salad plates and spoon the corn salad on top. Garnish each plate with goat cheese and serve.

Sugar Snap Pea and Soft Goat Cheese Salad with Cornbread Muffins

Serves 6 (makes about ¾ cup dressing and 12 muffins)

The combination of cornbread, sweet wildflower honey, and fresh goat cheese hits on classic American flavors for me. These flavors complement the young, green quality of the sugar snap peas and pea shoots you'll find at farmers' markets in early spring. This recipe also gifts you with extra cornbread muffins; freeze them for another day or eat them as a snack.

This dressing is as simple as they get but might require a hunt for the sweet, fruity moscato vinegar. Look for it at a specialty grocer or gourmet food shop, or, if you have to, use apple cider vinegar in its place. —AS

Cornbread

Nonstick cooking spray

1 cup (5 ounces/144 grams) all-purpose flour

1 cup (5.5 ounces/160 grams) coarsely ground cornmeal

⅓ cup (2.5 ounces/71 grams) packed light brown sugar

2 teaspoons baking powder

1 teaspoon kosher salt

½ teaspoon baking soda

1¼ cups low-fat buttermilk

2 large eggs

¼ cup vegetable oil

Honey, for serving

Sugar Snap Pea and Soft Goat Cheese Salad

½ cup extra-virgin olive oil

¼ cup moscato vinegar

½ teaspoon finely chopped fresh thyme

Kosher salt

½ pound sugar snap peas

1 bunch pea shoots (about 4 ounces)

6 ounces fresh goat cheese

1. **Make the cornbread:** Arrange a rack in the center of the oven and preheat the oven to 375°F. Coat a 12-cup muffin pan with nonstick cooking spray.

2. In a large bowl, combine the flour, cornmeal, sugar, baking powder, salt, and baking soda and whisk to combine. In a medium bowl, combine the buttermilk, eggs, and vegetable oil and whisk to combine. Using your hand, make a well in the middle of the cornmeal mixture and pour the buttermilk mixture into it. Using a rubber spatula, stir to combine.

3. Gently scoop the batter into the muffin cups, dividing it equally and filling each one about three-quarters full. Bake for 15 minutes or until a tester stick inserted into the center of a muffin comes out clean. Set the muffins aside to cool in the pan.

4. **Make the sugar snap pea and goat cheese salad:** In a small bowl or glass measuring cup, combine the olive oil, vinegar, and thyme and whisk to combine. Season with salt and set aside.

5. Fill a large bowl with ice and water. Bring a medium pot of water to a boil. Add the snap peas and cook until crisp-tender, about 2 minutes. Using a slotted spoon, transfer the snap peas to the ice water bath to stop cooking. Drain the snap peas and set aside.

6. In a large bowl, combine the snap peas with the pea shoots. Spoon the vinaigrette over the top, using as much as you desire, and toss gently to incorporate. (Reserve any remaining vinaigrette for another use. Stored in an airtight container in the refrigerator, it will keep for up to 2 weeks.)

7. Divide the salad among six small salad plates. Garnish the salads with the goat cheese. Place a cornbread muffin in the center of the salad on each plate. (Reserve the remaining muffins for another use.) Lightly drizzle honey over the cornbread and serve.

Melon Salad with Arugula, Fennel, and Marjoram

Serves 4

The combination of melon, marjoram, and sweet moscato vinegar in this delicate salad tastes like summer to me. When I serve guests this dish, I like to watch them take their first bite and enjoy a moment of pure bliss as the melon juices run down their chin.

I use heirloom Canary, Charentais, and watermelons from the farmers' market in this dish, but you could substitute more common melon varieties like cantaloupe and honeydew. Using a combination of different colored melons brings a pleasing aesthetic to the dish. You can also swap mint or torn basil leaves for the marjoram or use a few fistfuls of mizuna instead of arugula to switch up the salad throughout melon season. Look for moscato vinegar at a specialty grocery or gourmet food shop. Its sweet, fruity flavor makes it worth the hunt, though you can substitute apple cider vinegar if needed. —AS

½ medium Canary melon, rind removed and flesh cut into ½-inch pieces (about 3½ cups)

½ medium Charentais melon, rind removed and flesh cut into ½-inch pieces (about 3½ cups)

¼ small heirloom watermelon, rind removed and flesh cut into ½-inch pieces (about 1 cup)

1 teaspoon kosher salt, plus more for seasoning

1 medium fennel bulb, thinly sliced

3 tablespoons extra-virgin olive oil

1½ tablespoons moscato vinegar

2 loosely packed cups baby arugula

2 tablespoons fresh marjoram, large leaves torn

1. In a large bowl, combine the Canary and Charentais melons and watermelon. Sprinkle with the salt and toss to combine.

2. Add the fennel to the bowl. Drizzle the oil and vinegar over the melons and fennel and gently mix with your hands. Let the melon and fennel marinate in the dressing at room temperature for 10 minutes.

3. Add the arugula and marjoram to the bowl and toss until just combined. Season with salt. Transfer the salad to a large rimmed serving platter or shallow salad bowl. Pour any juice from the bowl over the top of the salad and dig in.

Crispy Pig's Ear Salad with Ranch Dressing

Serves 4

This salad has a real yin-yang thing going for it. I've taken pig's ears, an offcut that most people think of as brutish, and fried them to make them both more approachable and more indulgent. Then I pile the fried strips on top of a delicate raw vegetable salad that provides a cool, crunchy contrast to the fatty ears. A squirt of creamy ranch dressing finishes the dish off.

If you don't want to bother making the salad, the fried pig's ear strips also make a great snack served with a ramekin of ranch for dipping on the side. —AS

Crispy Pig's Ears

3 (12-ounce) pig's ears, rinsed and scrubbed

3 tablespoons unsalted butter

1 medium leek, halved lengthwise, thinly sliced and rinsed well

1 medium fennel bulb, thinly sliced

4 garlic cloves, finely chopped

½ cup dry white wine, such as Chardonnay

2 tablespoons whole black peppercorns

2 tablespoons ground coriander

2 tablespoons ground fennel seed

2 tablespoons lemon pepper

2 tablespoons kosher salt

2 tablespoons finely chopped fresh thyme

1 quart chicken stock

1 cup low-fat buttermilk

4 cups lard, for frying

Seasoned Flour

3 cups all-purpose flour

2 tablespoons lemon pepper

1 tablespoon garlic powder

1 tablespoon kosher salt

1 tablespoon onion powder

2 teaspoons ground celery seed

Salad and Vinaigrette

4 medium radishes, thinly sliced

3 baby Chioggia beets, peeled and thinly sliced

1 medium English cucumber, peeled and thinly sliced

1 medium fennel bulb, thinly sliced

¼ head frisée

¼ cup fresh flat-leaf parsley

¼ cup extra-virgin olive oil

Finely grated zest and freshly squeezed juice of 1 lemon

Finely grated zest and freshly squeezed juice of 1 orange

1 teaspoon kosher salt, plus more for seasoning

1 teaspoon finely chopped fresh thyme

Ranch Dressing (page 86), for serving

1. **Make the crispy pig's ears:** Arrange a rack in the center of the oven and preheat the oven to 375°F. Arrange the pig's ears in a 9 by 13-inch baking pan and set aside.

2. In a medium saucepan set over medium-high heat, warm the butter until it melts. Add the leek and sliced fennel and cook, stirring occasionally, until translucent, about 5 minutes. Add the garlic and cook, stirring occasionally, until fragrant and lightly browned, about 1 minute more.

3. Add the wine, peppercorns, coriander, fennel seed, lemon pepper, salt, and thyme to the saucepan. Bring the mixture to a simmer and cook, stirring occasionally, until the vegetables have absorbed the wine, about 5 minutes. Add the stock, return the mixture to a simmer, and cook for 5 minutes more. Pour the stock over the pig's ears, cover with aluminum foil, and transfer to the oven to cook for 2 hours or until fork-tender. Remove the pan from the oven. Remove the pig's ears from the stock, scraping any spices that cling to them back into the pan. Transfer the pig's ears to a cutting board to cool completely. (Discard the stock and aromatics.)

4. **Meanwhile, make the seasoned flour:** In a large bowl, combine the flour, lemon pepper, garlic powder, salt, onion powder, and celery seed and whisk to combine. Set aside.

5. Using a chef's knife, cut the pig's ears into ¼-inch-thick strips. In a large bowl, combine the strips with the buttermilk and let soak for 15 minutes at room temperature. Line a large baking sheet with paper towels and set aside.

6. **Meanwhile, make the salad and vinaigrette:** In a large bowl, combine the radishes, beets, cucumber, sliced fennel, frisée, and parsley and toss to combine. In a small bowl or glass measuring cup, combine the oil with the lemon zest, lemon juice, orange zest, and orange juice, and whisk to combine. Add the salt and thyme and whisk to combine. Set the salad and vinaigrette aside.

7. In a 12-inch cast-iron skillet set over medium-high heat, warm the lard until it reaches 350°F on a deep-frying thermometer. Drain the pig's ear strips. Working in batches, dredge the strips and place them in the skillet; do not crowd the skillet. Fry the strips until crispy and golden brown, turning halfway through, about 3 minutes. Transfer the fried strips to the paper towel–lined baking sheet to drain. Repeat the process with the remaining pig's ear strips. Discard any remaining flour mixture.

8. Pour the vinaigrette over the salad to taste and toss to combine. Season with salt. Divide the salad among four salad plates. Divide the fried pig's ear strips among the salads, laying them on top of the vegetables. Squirt or drizzle ranch dressing over the salads and dig in.

Ranch Dressing

Makes 2 cups

When in doubt, I say serve it with ranch. I serve the staple American dressing on the side of raw vegetables, chicken wings, spooned on top of salads and burgers, and with anything fried—onion rings, fried chicken, fried pig's ears, you name it. It's a great flavor vehicle and as true an American condiment as they come. Making it yourself rather than relying on a store-bought bottle of dressing lends a really personal touch to your meals. —AS

2 large egg yolks

1 tablespoon apple cider vinegar

1½ teaspoons freshly squeezed lemon juice

1 cup vegetable oil

¾ cup full-fat sour cream

½ cup low-fat buttermilk

1½ teaspoons lemon pepper

1¼ teaspoons kosher salt, plus more for seasoning

¾ teaspoon dried thyme

½ teaspoon garlic powder

½ teaspoon onion powder

½ teaspoon sugar

¼ teaspoon ground celery seed

1. In the bowl of a stand mixer fitted with the whisk attachment, combine the egg yolks, vinegar, and lemon juice and whisk on medium speed to combine. With the motor running, slowly add the oil to create an emulsion. (You can also combine the ingredients in a medium bowl and whisk them by hand to create the mayonnaise base. It should be fairly thick.)

2. Add the sour cream, buttermilk, lemon pepper, salt, thyme, garlic powder, onion powder, sugar, and celery seed and whisk on low speed to incorporate. Season with salt. Stored in an airtight container in the refrigerator, the dressing will keep for up to 5 days.

MY HOMAGE TO RANCH

I have a not-so-secret love for ranch dressing. Regardless of the meal, I'm always reaching for the stuff. If it's a burger, it needs ranch. If it's grilled chicken, I go for ranch. If it's a big bowl of potato chips, it's always ranch. As far as I'm concerned, it's the top-of-the-heap dressing, spread, dip, and sauce.

There's no other dressing in the whole wide world that screams "America" to me more than ranch, which has its roots in the soul of the heartland. More than sixty years ago, Nebraska native Steve Henson and his high school sweetheart, Gayle, moved west to sunny Santa Barbara, California, hoping to get rich running a little guest ranch in Hidden Valley. They struck gold with a homemade buttermilk salad dressing that they made for guests and later started shipping to fans across the country. It was the original ranch.

Before bottled ranch dressing became a household staple, Mr. Henson sold a spice packet that contained the secret mix of herbs and seasonings he used to make the dressing from scratch. Home cooks just had to add buttermilk and sour cream, and the dressing was good to go. Growing up, my mom bought that spice packet often and always followed the directions to a T. She'd serve it with chips or douse iceberg lettuce and pickles with the creamy goodness and call it her afternoon snack.

At The Country Cat, we like to create our own versions of classic American salad bar dressings. Ranch is my favorite (see page 86). Jackie and I tasted the packaged version countless times in order to replicate the tang, texture, and distinct blend of herbs that taps into that taste memory from childhood and keeps us coming back for more. We think the spice blend we created comes pretty close to the original—and it couldn't be easier to make.

When we've got a batch of homemade ranch on hand, we throw it on cold, crisp salads, use it as a garnish for grilled meats, and serve it as a dip for anything and everything. My favorite use, though, has got to be as a dip for chips, cut with a generous shot of Sriracha. (We call my special blend "SriRancha" at the Sappington house.) You can use the dressing however you want, but know that once you experience the virtues of making your own ranch, a jar of this addictive stuff will always be a fixture in your fridge. —AS

Asparagus and Wild Rice Soup with Parsley Lemon Garlic Butter, page 92

THE KETTLE

Early in my cooking career, I had to make ten gallons of soup every morning and come up with a new soup to serve every other day. Needless to say, I've spent a considerable amount of time in the kitchen thinking about the most effective ways to build and enhance the flavor of a soup's ingredients while still paying them proper respect. In the end, my soup-making approach boils down to two methods. In all the soups I make, I either expand the flavor profiles of the ingredients by adding stock or cream and turning them into an elegant pureed soup, or make a chunky, hearty soup that keeps the ingredients in their simplest form to preserve their integrity in the bowl. —AS

Asparagus and Wild Rice Soup with Parsley Lemon Garlic Butter

Serves 4 to 6

When the first stalks of asparagus come into season in the spring, I like to combine them with earthy wild rice in this light soup. An easy compound butter flavored with parsley, lemon, and garlic acts as the garnish and gives the soup a bright, citrusy flavor. —AS

Parsley Lemon Garlic Butter

2 tablespoons unsalted butter, at room temperature

2 tablespoons finely chopped fresh flat-leaf parsley

Finely grated zest of 2 lemons

½ garlic clove, finely chopped

Asparagus and Wild Rice Soup

½ cup wild rice

1½ teaspoons unsalted butter

1½ teaspoons extra-virgin olive oil

2 medium carrots, peeled, trimmed, and finely chopped

1 large celery stalk, peeled, trimmed, and finely chopped (see Chef's Note)

½ medium yellow onion, finely chopped

4 garlic cloves, thinly sliced

1 tablespoon finely chopped fresh thyme

½ teaspoon chili flakes

1 dried bay leaf

Finely grated zest and freshly squeezed juice of ½ lemon

½ cup dry white wine, such as Chardonnay

1 quart chicken stock

¾ pound asparagus, trimmed and cut into ½-inch pieces

Kosher salt

1. **Make the parsley lemon garlic butter:** In a small bowl, combine the butter, parsley, lemon zest, and garlic and, using a rubber spatula, mix to combine. Transfer the bowl to the refrigerator until ready to use.

2. **Make the asparagus and wild rice soup:** In a small saucepan, combine the wild rice with 2 cups water. Bring the mixture to a boil, then reduce the heat to low and simmer until the rice is tender and has absorbed all the water, about 45 minutes. Remove the pot from the heat, cover, and set aside.

3. Meanwhile, in a medium stockpot set over medium-low heat, combine the butter, oil, and ¼ cup water and cook until the butter has melted and the water, butter, and oil combine. Add the carrots, celery, and onion and stir to combine. Cover the pot and cook, stirring occasionally, until the vegetables have softened, about 15 minutes.

4. Add the garlic, thyme, chili flakes, bay leaf, lemon zest, and lemon juice to the pot and stir to combine. Cover and cook, stirring occasionally, until the garlic is fragrant and lightly browned, about 3 minutes. Stir in the wine, raise the heat to medium-high, and cook, stirring occasionally, until the aromatics absorb all of the wine, about 5 minutes more.

5. Add the stock to the pot and bring the soup to a rolling simmer. Add the asparagus and turn off the heat. Remove and discard the bay leaf. Stir in the rice. Season with salt. Ladle the soup into four to six shallow soup bowls and top each bowl with a dollop of the herb butter. Serve.

Chef's Note: To peel the fibrous strings off a celery stalk, trim the top and bottom off the stalk. Hold the stalk vertically over a cutting board and place a vegetable peeler against the outside of the stalk. Then run the peeler down the length of the stalk, like you would when peeling a carrot, to remove the strings.

Stewed Red Potato, Baby Squash, and Sweet Onion Soup with Walnut Pistou

Serves 6 to 8 (makes about 1 cup pistou)

This brothy soup is deceptively hearty and just the recipe for a rainy spring day. The onions and fennel give the soup a slightly sweet flavor that I like to offset with chili flakes, fresh herbs, and a dollop of black walnut pistou. Black walnuts are a Midwest favorite, but they can be hard to find in other parts of the country, so I've called for regular walnuts in this recipe. Go ahead and substitute an equal amount of black walnuts if you can find them, because their bitter flavor goes well with the soup. You'll have extra pistou; I like to use the leftovers as a pasta sauce. —AS

Walnut Pistou

1 cup walnuts, toasted (see Chef's Note, page 55)

¾ cup extra-virgin olive oil

3 garlic cloves

1 teaspoon kosher salt, plus more for seasoning

Finely grated zest of 1 lemon

3 cups lightly packed fresh flat-leaf parsley

¼ cup finely grated Parmesan cheese

Stewed Red Potato, Baby Squash, and Sweet Onion Soup

6 cups vegetable stock

2 tablespoons extra-virgin olive oil

1½ large sweet onions, such as Walla Wallas, finely chopped

1½ teaspoons kosher salt, plus more for seasoning

5 garlic cloves, thinly sliced

½ large fennel bulb, finely chopped

4 medium red potatoes, cut into ½-inch pieces

1½ teaspoons chili flakes

Finely grated zest of 1 lemon

Freshly ground black pepper

4 baby squash, such as crookneck, zucchini, or pattypan squash, cut into coins and halved

Freshly squeezed juice of ½ lemon

1 tablespoon finely chopped fresh oregano

1 tablespoon finely chopped fresh flat-leaf parsley

1 tablespoon finely chopped fresh thyme

1. **Make the walnut pistou:** In a blender or the bowl of a food processor fitted with the steel blade, combine the walnuts, oil, garlic, salt, and lemon zest. With the motor running, blend the mixture while adding small handfuls of the parsley at a time. Continue blending until you have added all the parsley and the mixture becomes a loose pesto, about 1 minute. Add the cheese to the mixture and blend until just combined. Season with additional salt and set aside.

2. **Make the stewed red potato, baby squash, and sweet onion soup:** In a large lidded pot set over medium heat, warm ¼ cup of the stock and the oil. Stir in the onions and salt. Cover the pot and cook, stirring occasionally, until the onions are translucent, about 8 minutes. Remove the lid and stir in the garlic. Cover and cook, stirring occasionally, until the garlic is soft and translucent, about 3 minutes. Add the fennel, cover, and cook, stirring occasionally, until the fennel is soft and translucent, about 3 minutes.

3. Add the potatoes, 2 cups of the stock, chili flakes, and lemon zest to the pot. Season with salt and pepper, then raise the heat to high and bring the soup to a simmer. Reduce the heat to medium and simmer for 5 minutes.

4. Stir in the squash, remaining 3¾ cups stock, and lemon juice, then raise the heat to high and bring the soup to a simmer. Reduce the heat to medium and simmer until the squash and potatoes are fork-tender but not yet splitting, about 10 minutes.

5. Remove the soup from the heat and stir in the oregano, parsley, and thyme. Season with additional salt and pepper. Divide the soup among six to eight bowls and garnish each serving with 1 tablespoon of the pistou. (Reserve any remaining pistou for another use. Stored in an airtight container, the pistou will keep for up to 3 days in the refrigerator or up to 1 week in the freezer.) Dig in.

Stewed Red Potato, Baby Squash, and Sweet Onion Soup with Walnut Pistou, page 98

Smoked Tomato Soup, page 102

Smoked Tomato Soup

Serves 4 to 6

We pair this smoky spin on a classic American soup with a hearty grilled cheese and lightly dressed green salad at the restaurant. Smoking the tomatoes lends the soup a depth of flavor that goes nicely with the rich, molten cheese in the sandwich. Served with a sandwich or on its own, this soup is an ideal rainy-day lunch.

If you don't have access to a smoker, you can skip step 1 to make this tomato soup with plain canned tomatoes and still get great results. —AS

2 cups hickory chips, for smoking

1 (28-ounce) can whole peeled or diced tomatoes, with their juices

5 allspice berries

5 whole cloves

1 dried bay leaf

1 tablespoon whole black peppercorns

1 tablespoon ground coriander

3 tablespoons extra-virgin olive oil

1 medium yellow onion, finely chopped

1 medium fennel bulb, finely chopped

4 garlic cloves, finely chopped

¼ teaspoon chili flakes

¼ cup red wine vinegar

2 tablespoons tomato paste

2 tablespoons herbes de Provence (without lavender)

2 teaspoons kosher salt, plus more for seasoning

½ cup dry white wine, such as Chardonnay

½ cup heavy cream

4 to 6 tablespoons sour cream

1. Soak the wood chips according to package instructions and preheat a smoker to 225°F. (Or see "Smoking Without a Smoker," page 35.) Place the wet hickory chips over the fire or in an electric hopper. Place the tomatoes in a stainless-steel, nonreactive roasting pan and smoke for 1 hour 30 minutes. (This step can be done a day ahead.)

2. Spread a 4-inch square piece of cheesecloth out on a clean work surface and place the allspice berries, cloves, bay leaf, black peppercorns, and coriander in the center. Bring the corners of the cheesecloth together and tie the ends with a length of butcher's twine, making sure the cloth is secure and no spices will escape. Set aside the spice sachet.

3. When the tomatoes are ready, in a large saucepan set over medium heat, warm the oil. Add the onion, fennel, garlic, chili flakes, and ½ cup water and cook, stirring occasionally, until the vegetables are soft and translucent,

about 5 minutes. Add the vinegar, tomato paste, herbes de Provence, and salt and stir to incorporate. (The mixture will look a little pasty and thick.) Add the wine and cook, stirring occasionally, for 5 minutes more.

4. Reduce the heat to low, add the smoked tomatoes, spice sachet, and 2 cups water, and cook for 30 minutes more. Remove the saucepan from the heat and let the soup cool for 15 minutes.

5. Remove the sachet from the soup and discard. Working in batches, in a blender or the bowl of a food processor fitted with the steel blade, puree the soup until smooth. (It should coat, not cake, the back of a spoon.) Return the soup to the pot. (Alternatively, puree the soup directly in the pot using an immersion blender.) Add the cream and stir to combine. Season with salt. Divide the soup among four to six bowls, garnish each bowl with 1 tablespoon of sour cream, and dig in.

Creamy Celery Root Soup

Serves 4 to 6

The clean white flesh of celery root brings a real elegance to the table each winter. I like to simmer it in milk and puree it to create a deceptively simple soup that's worth breaking out the fancy china for. Though this soup is delicious on its own, you can also garnish it with shaved white or black truffles or rye bread croutons if you like.

When you're simmering the soup, the milk will likely look curdled and broken. This is actually caused by elements that the celery root releases during the cooking process and isn't something to worry about. —AS

1 tablespoon unsalted butter

½ medium fennel bulb, roughly chopped

½ medium yellow onion, roughly chopped

1 garlic clove, finely chopped

1½ teaspoons finely chopped fresh sage leaves

1½ teaspoons finely chopped fresh thyme

½ teaspoon chili flakes

½ medium celery root, peeled and cut into ½-inch pieces

1½ teaspoons kosher salt, plus more for seasoning

4 cups whole milk

Finely grated zest of ½ lemon

Freshly squeezed juice of ¼ lemon, plus more for seasoning

1. In a large saucepan set over medium-high heat, combine the butter with 1 tablespoon water and warm until the butter has melted and the water and butter combine. Add the fennel, onion, garlic, sage, thyme, and chili flakes, cover, and cook, stirring occasionally, until the vegetables are translucent, about 5 minutes.

2. Add the celery root, salt, and milk, cover, and bring the mixture to a simmer. Simmer, stirring occasionally, until you can easily mash the celery root with a fork, about 35 minutes.

3. Remove the saucepan from the heat and stir in the lemon zest and lemon juice. Let the soup cool for 30 minutes.

4. Working in batches, in a blender or the bowl of a food processor fitted with the steel blade, puree the soup until smooth. (It should coat, not cake, the back of a spoon.) Return the soup to the pan. (Alternatively, puree the soup directly in the pan using an immersion blender.) Season with salt and additional lemon juice.

5. Return the soup to the stove and reheat over medium heat until warm. Divide the soup among four to six bowls and dig in.

Autumn Squash Soup with Apple Cider and Brown Butter

Serves 4 to 6

Autumn squash epitomizes the flavor of fall for me, especially when I'm cooking with heirloom squash varieties like kabocha. This soup combines the deep orange flesh of the green-skinned kabocha with nutty brown butter, fresh-pressed apple cider, and maple syrup to create a sweet-savory soup that's as beautiful as any fall scene. This soup is great served solo, but you can also garnish it with toasted pumpkin seeds, roasted mushrooms, thinly sliced apples, or brioche croutons, if you like. —AS

1 (2½-pound) kabocha squash, halved and seeded

6 tablespoons (¾ stick) unsalted butter, cut into ½-inch cubes

2 cups unsweetened apple cider

1 firm, crisp medium apple, such as Honeycrisp, peeled, cored, and quartered

½ large yellow onion, thinly sliced

½ medium fennel bulb, thinly sliced

2 tablespoons apple cider vinegar, plus more for seasoning

2 garlic cloves, finely chopped

1 tablespoon finely chopped fresh sage leaves

1 tablespoon finely chopped fresh thyme

1 tablespoon pure maple syrup

Kosher salt and freshly ground black pepper

1. Arrange a rack in the center of the oven and preheat the oven to 400°F. Line a large baking sheet with parchment paper and place the squash, cut-side down, on the pan. Roast for 1 hour or until tender when pierced with a fork. Let cool slightly, then peel away and discard the skin and any other tough pieces. (You should have about 2½ cups squash flesh.)

2. Meanwhile, in a medium Dutch oven set over medium heat, melt the butter. Cook, whisking frequently, until the butter solids are brown and start to smell nutty, about 5 minutes.

3. Add the apple cider, apple, onion, fennel, vinegar, sage, thyme, and maple syrup and bring the mixture to a simmer. Season with salt and pepper. Reduce the heat to low, cover, and cook until the apples, fennel, and onion are soft and tender, about 30 minutes. Add the squash to the soup and cook for 10 minutes more to blend the flavors. Let the soup cool for 30 minutes.

4. Working in batches, in a blender or the bowl of a food processor fitted with the steel blade, puree the soup until smooth. (It should coat, not cake, the back of a spoon.)

Return the soup to the pot. (Alternatively, puree the soup directly in the pot using an immersion blender.) If the soup is too thick, add water until you've reached the desired consistency. Season with salt and pepper and additional vinegar, if desired.

5. Return the soup to the stove and reheat over medium heat until warm. Divide the soup among four to six bowls and dig in.

Mama's Chili

Serves 6 to 8

When I make chili at home, I use ground turkey to balance out all the red meat in our life. This chili is great right from the pot but even better if you make it a day ahead and give the flavors more time to develop. I like to serve big bowls to Adam and our boys, with cornbread or tortilla chips alongside. If you don't have time to soak the dried beans, you can substitute two 14.5-ounce cans of each bean in a pinch. —JS

½ pound dried kidney beans

½ pound dried pinto beans

3 tablespoons kosher salt,
plus more for seasoning

2 tablespoons extra-virgin olive oil

1½ pounds ground dark turkey meat

1 medium yellow onion, finely chopped

3 garlic cloves, finely chopped

Freshly ground black pepper

1½ cups fresh or frozen corn kernels

¼ cup chili powder

1 tablespoon ground coriander

1 tablespoon ground cumin

1 tablespoon garlic powder

1 tablespoon onion powder

1 tablespoon sweet paprika

2 (14.5-ounce) cans diced tomatoes,
with their juices

2 cups chicken stock

Tabasco sauce (optional)

½ cup fresh cilantro leaves

½ cup full-fat sour cream

1. The day before serving, sort through the kidney and pinto beans and get rid of any rocks. In a large bowl, combine the beans with enough cold water to cover by 2 inches and soak overnight.

2. The next day, drain the beans and transfer them to a large stockpot. Fill the stockpot with enough water to cover the beans by 2 inches. Season the water with the salt and bring to a simmer. Cook the beans, stirring occasionally, until tender but not falling apart, 1 hour 30 minutes to 2 hours. Drain the beans and set aside.

3. In a large stockpot set over medium heat, warm the oil. Add the turkey, onion, and garlic and season with salt and pepper. Cook, stirring occasionally to break up the turkey, until the meat is browned and the onions are translucent, about 10 minutes.

4. Add the corn, chili powder, coriander, cumin, garlic powder, onion powder, and paprika and stir to incorporate. Cook, stirring occasionally, until the spices are well incorporated and the corn starts to soften, about 5 minutes. Add the beans and stir to combine. Add the diced tomatoes with their juices and the stock and stir to combine. Bring the chili to a gentle simmer and cook, stirring occasionally, until the flavors taste nicely melded together, 1 hour 30 minutes to 2 hours. (If the chili is sticking and scorching on the bottom of the pot, reduce the heat slightly.) Add Tabasco for extra heat, if desired.

5. Scoop the chili into six to eight soup bowls, garnish with the cilantro and sour cream, and dig in.

LET IT SWEAT

Making soup is more than just throwing ingredients into a pot and topping them with water, stock, or cream. It's about finding the most effective way to build and expand the flavors of the ingredients you're using. Whether I'm making chunky soup or pureed soup, I always start the soup-making process by sweating a distinct mix of aromatic vegetables in a mixture of fat and water. Most people cook these aromatics in a tiny bit of fat for just a few minutes, then add a broth or other liquid to the soup base too early in the process. I've learned that these aromatics need more time on the stove to let their flavors bloom.

The flavor base I've come to call my own always starts with a combination of onions, leeks, fennel, garlic, chili flakes, fresh thyme, lemon zest, lemon juice, dry white wine, and stock. I cook these ingredients in unsalted butter or extra-virgin olive oil or a combination of the two fats. If I want sweetness and creaminess in a soup, then it's butter all the way. When I'm after a little acidity and a soup with strong savory appeal, I use olive oil. If I'm looking for the best of both worlds, I combine the two fats. With regard to the recipes in this book, I add about ¼ cup of water to the pan to help stabilize the temperature of the fats and facilitate the sweating process. After I add the water, I swirl the pan to create an emulsion. I call this home for the aromatics to start their sweat.

Cooking the ingredients low and slow is essential for building bold flavors in all of my soups. It's a simple method that produces consistently good soups. I add the onions, leeks, and fennel first, then cover the pot and let them sweat over medium heat until they're translucent and soft. Next, I add the lemon zest, lemon juice, spices, and garlic to the mix. This brings roundness to the vegetable base by adding acidity and the floral notes of the lemon. I treat the garlic like a spice as it provides depth of flavor to the mixture. Then I add the wine and let it reduce so the vegetables drink it up. The wine helps break the vegetables down and truly infuses the soup with concentrated flavors. At this point, you have a flavorful canvas on which to create a soup of your choice. —AS

FINGER FOODS

Sometimes silverware just gets in the way. When you have friends over for a cocktail party or an afternoon BBQ, it's nice to have some snacks out so people can walk by a table and graze with ease. Or have some small bites cooking on the grill that can quickly transfer to someone's hands and into their mouth. We love to put a few chilled finger foods out on the table before folks arrive, and then cook and socialize while bringing different waves of small plates to the table. It helps keep the party moving. —AS and JS

"Eat a Dozen" Deviled Eggs

Makes 24 deviled eggs

My mom made deviled eggs for every gathering at our house. My brother, Eric, and I always competed to see who could eat the most eggs the fastest. By the time we hit our twelfth deviled egg, we knew we'd overdone it, but we loved those eggs so much that we repeated the contest every chance we got.

The filling for these deviled eggs was inspired by my family recipe. But I take a different approach when it comes to how I handle the whites. Before filling the egg whites, I soak them in lemon water for a few hours to preserve them a bit and reduce their sulfurous flavor. You can skip this step, but I recommend trying it at least once. You'll get a cleaner, purer deviled egg for mere minutes of work. —AS

12 large eggs

Kosher salt

1 lemon, halved

2 tablespoons olive juice (from a can of olives)

1 tablespoon Dijon mustard

1 tablespoon mayonnaise

½ teaspoon ground celery seed

½ teaspoon sweet paprika, plus more for garnish

Freshly ground black pepper

1. Place the eggs in a medium saucepan and add cold water to completely cover the eggs. Salt the water and bring to a hard simmer over medium-high heat. Once the water reaches a hard simmer, cook the eggs for 9 minutes.

2. Drain the water, transfer the eggs to a colander, and run cool water over them. While they are still hot, peel the eggs one by one under cool running water.

3. Halve the eggs lengthwise. Remove the yolks and place them in the bowl of a food processor fitted with the steel blade. Place the whites in a large bowl and cover with 8 cups cold water. Squeeze the lemon halves into the water, then place the squeezed lemon halves in the water as well. Refrigerate the egg whites for 2 hours or up to 2 days.

4. Meanwhile, add the olive juice, mustard, mayonnaise, celery seed, and paprika to the yolks in the food processor. Pulse to make a smooth paste. Season with salt and pepper, transfer to an airtight container, and refrigerate until ready to use.

5. When the egg whites are ready, gently remove them from the lemon water, gently blot them dry with paper towels, and arrange them on a large serving platter. Spoon the yolk mixture into a pastry bag fitted with a large star tip. Tighten the bag to release any air pockets. Gently pipe the yolks into the egg whites. (Alternatively, you can spoon the filling into the egg whites for a more rustic look.) Garnish with a sprinkling of paprika and dig in.

Soft Buttery Pretzels

Makes 12 pretzels

When it comes to bar bites, nothing goes better with a cold beer than my warm buttery pretzels and a ramekin of hot mustard for dipping. I discovered the original recipe for these pretzels in Bernard Clayton's *Complete Book of Breads* many years ago and have since tweaked it to make it my own. Malt powder gives the dough a hint of complexity, while using baking soda in the boil lends the pretzels their golden color. Look for malt powder at a brewing supply store. —JS

5 cups (25 ounces/713 grams) all-purpose flour, plus more as needed

¼ cup kosher salt, plus more for garnish

3 tablespoons granulated sugar

1½ tablespoons malt powder

¾ teaspoon active dry yeast

Nonstick cooking spray

2 tablespoons baking soda

3 tablespoons unsalted butter, melted

Hot mustard, for serving

1. In the bowl of a stand mixer fitted with the dough hook, combine the flour, 1 tablespoon of the salt, the sugar, malt powder, and yeast and mix on low speed to combine. With the motor running, add 2 cups hot water. (The temperature of the water should read 110°F on a digital thermometer.) Mix until combined and the dough pulls away from the sides of the bowl and is supple and smooth but not tight, about 10 minutes. (The dough should not be overly wet, but will be slightly sticky. If the dough seems too wet, sprinkle a little additional flour into the bowl and mix for a few minutes longer.)

2. Grease a large bowl with nonstick cooking spray, turn the dough into the bowl, and cover with plastic wrap. Let the dough rest in a warm place for 15 minutes.

3. Turn the dough out onto a clean, lightly floured work surface and divide it into twelve equal portions. Cover the dough with a damp towel and let rest for 10 minutes.

4. Line a large baking sheet with parchment paper and grease the parchment paper with nonstick cooking spray. Working with one portion of the dough at a time, use both hands to roll the dough into an even rope about 12 inches long. Take the ends of the rope, bring them to the center, and twist to make an oblong pretzel with a twist in the middle. Press the tips together at the bottom of the pretzel, letting the ends flair out to the sides. Place the pretzel on the prepared baking sheet and repeat with the remaining dough.

5. Meanwhile, arrange a rack in the center of the oven and preheat the oven to 400°F. Fill a large stockpot with about 6 inches of water. Bring the water to a simmer, then add the remaining 3 tablespoons salt and the baking soda.

6. Place four pretzels in the simmering water and boil the pretzels until they rise to the surface. (If they don't rise immediately, you can nudge them with a wooden spoon to help them float.) Once the pretzels float, use a strainer to transfer them to the baking sheet. Repeat the process until all the pretzels are boiled. Transfer the pretzels to the oven and bake for 20 to 25 minutes or until golden brown.

7. Remove the pretzels from the oven and immediately brush them with the butter and sprinkle with salt. Transfer the pretzels to a large plate and serve with a ramekin filled with mustard on the side for dipping.

Judy

Makes about 3 cups

Though this family recipe is similar to a pimento or potted cheese, the Sappington family version is called Judy. Family legend has it that my grandpa Sappy coined the name, though no one really knows who the true Judy was.

I serve Judy as a bar snack with crackers and on top of our burger at The Cat, but actually think its best use is as picnic food. When preparing Judy at home, make sure you hand grate the cheese and use Budweiser beer. Finally, know that Judy is best made several days in advance; her flavor only improves as she festers. —AS

1 pound sharp cheddar cheese, coarsely grated (about 4 cups)

¼ large yellow onion, coarsely grated

½ cup Budweiser beer

¼ cup mayonnaise

¼ cup olive juice (from a can of olives)

4 dashes Tabasco sauce

Kosher salt and freshly ground black pepper

Crackers, for serving

1. In the bowl of a stand mixer fitted with the paddle attachment, combine the cheese, onion, beer, mayonnaise, olive juice, Tabasco, and salt and pepper to taste. Mix on medium-low speed until soft and slightly creamy, about 5 minutes.

2. Transfer the Judy to an airtight container and refrigerate for at least 24 hours or up to 1 week. Bring the Judy to room temperature before transferring to a serving bowl and digging in with crackers.

Grilled Oysters with Homemade BBQ Sauce, page 122

Grilled Oysters with Homemade BBQ Sauce

Serves 4 (makes about 2 cups sauce)

Grilling oysters is a nice variation that lets you enjoy them in an outdoor setting. Grilled oysters pick up a bit of smoke, so pairing them with a homemade BBQ sauce is an obvious choice. In my BBQ sauce, I only use black pepper for heat because I'm looking for the warm background notes, not the hot upfront heat you would get from chiles or chili flakes.

When you are prepping the oysters, make sure to rinse them in a colander under cold water and, using a green scrubby pad, scrub and inspect each oyster for sand, dirt, seaweed, and crustaceans that have attached themselves to the shells. It's important to remove these elements to ensure a pleasant and enjoyable eating experience. —AS

BBQ Sauce

2 cups hickory chips, for smoking

1 (28-ounce) can unsalted whole peeled tomatoes or unsalted diced tomatoes, with their juices

½ medium yellow onion, thinly sliced

1 medium celery stalk, trimmed, peeled, and thinly sliced (see Chef's Note, page 93)

3 garlic cloves, thinly sliced

¼ cup packed light brown sugar

¼ cup unsulphured blackstrap molasses

¼ cup tomato paste

2 tablespoons red wine vinegar

2 tablespoons freshly ground black pepper, plus more for seasoning

1 tablespoon kosher salt, plus more for seasoning

1 tablespoon ground mustard seed

2 teaspoons ground celery seed

2 teaspoons garlic powder

2 teaspoons onion powder

Grilled Oysters

24 medium oysters in the shell, scrubbed

Kosher salt, for serving

1 lemon, halved

1. **Make the BBQ sauce:** Soak the wood chips according to package instructions and preheat a smoker to 225°F. (Or see "Smoking Without a Smoker," page 35.) Place the wet hickory chips over the fire or in an electric hopper. Place the tomatoes with their juices in a stainless-steel, nonreactive roasting pan and smoke for 1 hour 30 minutes. (This step can be done a day ahead.)

2. Arrange a rack in the center of the oven and preheat the oven to 400°F.

3. In a medium bowl, combine the smoked tomatoes, onion, celery, garlic, sugar, molasses, tomato paste, vinegar, pepper, salt, mustard seed, celery seed, garlic powder, and onion powder and stir to combine. Season to taste with salt and pepper to balance the salty-sweet flavors you want in a BBQ sauce. Pour the mixture into a 9-inch square baking pan and roast for 1 hour 30 minutes or until the top is caramelized and the sauce has reduced by about one-quarter to create deep, pronounced flavors.

4. Remove the BBQ sauce from the oven and let cool slightly. Season with salt and pepper and let cool for at least 1 hour at room temperature or cover and refrigerate for up to 1 day. Working in batches, in a blender or the bowl of a food processor fitted with the steel blade, puree the BBQ sauce until smooth, about 3 minutes. (Alternatively, puree the BBQ sauce directly in the pan using an immersion blender.) Transfer the BBQ sauce to an airtight container and set aside.

5. **Make the grilled oysters:** Prepare a hot fire in a charcoal grill. Arrange a grill grate 2 inches above the coals. Arrange the oysters on the grill grate over direct heat with the bowl side of the oysters over the heat, not the lid. Grill until the shells pop open and the juices are boiling hot, turning halfway through, 3 to 4 minutes per side. (Make sure to use a pair of tongs and a kitchen towel when turning the oysters and removing them from the grill. If the oysters don't pop open but the juices are spitting out of the side, this is an indicator that they are done as well. Remember, you don't want to overcook the oysters and boil all the water out, so plan on babysitting them.)

6. Transfer the oysters to a cutting board to cool slightly. Using an oyster shucker, unhinge the oyster shell and loosen the muscle from the shell. Place a pool of kosher salt on a large platter and place the oysters on the half shell on top of the salt. (This prevents the oysters from spilling or falling over.) Spoon about 1 tablespoon of the BBQ sauce onto each oyster. (Reserve the remaining BBQ sauce for another use. Stored in an airtight container in the refrigerator, it will keep for up to 3 weeks.) Squeeze the lemon over the whole plate of oysters and dig in.

Chef's Note: If you don't have access to a smoker, you can skip step 1 to make this BBQ sauce with plain canned tomatoes and still get great results.

Meat Candy (aka Beef Jerky)

Makes about ½ pound

Certain snacks make you feel like you have to have them now. No food is guiltier of that than the American staple, beef jerky. I fell in love with jerky when I was a kid in Missouri. Ever since, I've been fascinated with learning how to make my own. This recipe has salty-sweet notes and the hidden flavor of celery seed to put a personal stamp on what I feel is truly meat candy.

With its lean marble and defined grain, the eye of round off the cow works perfectly for jerky. Make sure to use a meat slicer or a very sharp knife to slice the beef consistently and paper-thin. When it comes to jerky, it's "thin to win," so you end up with not-too-chewy and perfectly seasoned pieces of beef. —AS

2 tablespoons packed light brown sugar

2 tablespoons kosher salt

1 tablespoon freshly ground black pepper

1 teaspoon ground celery seed

1 teaspoon chili flakes

1 pound eye of round beef, very thinly sliced

1. In a medium bowl, combine the sugar, salt, pepper, celery seed, and chili flakes and whisk to combine.

2. Working with one slice of beef at a time, dip the beef in the seasoning mixture to coat and cover each slice thoroughly. Place the slices on the drying racks of a food dehydrator and repeat until you have used all of the beef and seasoning.

3. Place the racks into the food dehydrator and set the temperature to 180°F. Dehydrate the beef for 12 hours or until it is dry and a little chewy. Stored in an airtight container at room temperature, the beef jerky will keep well for up to 1 month.

A Side of Love (Crispy Onion Rings)

Serves 4 to 6

I'm not a fan of big, thick onion rings because the batter always falls off. I'd rather slice sweet onions nice and thin on a mandoline (a sharp knife works, too), toss them in buttermilk and a simple seasoned flour, then fry them up to create crispy shoestring-style rings. Because we fry so many batches each day at the restaurant, our kitchen crew refers to this dish as "a side of love" to keep the mood light and airy, just like the rings themselves. Serve the rings as a side for steak or a brisket sandwich, on top of meat loaf, or piled high on a plate with Homemade Ketchup (page 128) on the side for dipping to bring genuine pleasure to the table. —AS

3 large Spanish or Walla Walla onions, cut into ⅛-inch-thick slices

1 cup low-fat buttermilk

3 cups all-purpose flour

1 tablespoon kosher salt, plus more for seasoning

6 cups vegetable oil

Homemade Ketchup (page 128), for dipping

1. In a large bowl, combine the onions with the butter-milk and use your hands to toss the onions, separating them into rings and making sure they are evenly coated with the buttermilk. Let the onions sit in the buttermilk at room temperature for 10 minutes or in the refrigerator for up to 1 hour.

2. In a separate large bowl, combine the flour with the salt and whisk to combine. Set aside.

3. In a medium stockpot or cast-iron Dutch oven set over medium-high heat, warm the vegetable oil until it reaches 350°F on a deep-frying thermometer. Meanwhile, preheat the oven to 250°F. Line a large baking sheet with paper towels.

4. Working in small batches, remove the onions from the bowl and gently shake off any excess buttermilk.

5. Place the onions in the bowl with the seasoned flour and use your hands to toss them in the flour mixture as if you were tossing a salad, lightly lifting and shaking the onions to coat them evenly and prevent clumping. Shake off any excess flour and immediately transfer the onions to the hot oil.

6. Fry the onions, stirring them occasionally with a fish fork or pair of tongs to make sure they fry evenly and adjusting the heat to maintain a steady temperature, until golden brown, about 2 minutes. Using a pair of tongs, transfer the fried onions to the paper towel–lined baking sheet. Season with salt, then keep warm in the oven while frying the remaining onions.

7. Transfer the onion rings to a large serving plate and serve with a ramekin filled with ketchup on the side for dipping.

Homemade Ketchup

Makes about 4 cups

I started making ketchup from scratch because I was curious about how it was made, and I wanted to put my personal stamp on the ketchup I serve with my Crispy Onion Rings (page 126) and crispy home fries (see Chef's Note, page 231). The final spice blend I decided to use in this ketchup came about through trial and error, as I searched for a combination that delivered bigger, bolder flavors than you'd taste in a mainstream brand.

Making your own ketchup helps you control every flavor element of a meal. It's also easy to make and keeps well, so you can make a batch over the weekend and spend the week slathering it on whatever you want. —AS

1 (28-ounce) can unsalted whole peeled tomatoes or unsalted diced tomatoes, with their juices

¼ cup tomato paste

2 tablespoons red wine vinegar

2 tablespoons distilled white vinegar

3 tablespoons packed light brown sugar

1 tablespoon granulated sugar

1 tablespoon kosher salt

2 teaspoons ground celery seed

2 teaspoons garlic powder

¼ teaspoon ground ginger

¼ teaspoon chili flakes

1 tablespoon vegetable oil

½ small yellow onion, finely chopped

4 allspice berries

4 juniper berries

1 whole clove

1 star anise

1 dried bay leaf

½ cinnamon stick

¼ teaspoon ground fennel seed

1 tablespoon cornstarch

1. In a large bowl, combine the tomatoes, tomato paste, red wine vinegar, distilled white vinegar, brown sugar, granulated sugar, salt, celery seed, garlic powder, ginger, chili flakes, and ¼ cup water and stir to combine. Set aside.

2. In a medium saucepan set over medium heat, warm the oil. Add the onion and cook, stirring occasionally, until lightly caramelized and translucent, about 5 minutes. Add the tomato mixture and stir to combine. Bring the mixture to a simmer.

3. Meanwhile, spread a 4-inch square piece of cheesecloth out on a clean work surface and place the allspice berries, juniper berries, clove, star anise, bay leaf, cinnamon stick, and fennel seed in the center. Bring the corners of the cheesecloth together and tie the ends with a length of butcher's twine, making sure the cloth is secure and no spices can escape. Add the spice sachet to the saucepan, reduce the heat to low, and simmer, stirring occasionally, until the tomatoes start to break down and the mixture has reduced by about one-third and is somewhat set, about 45 minutes.

4. Remove the tomato mixture from the heat and let cool for 30 minutes. Remove and discard the sachet. Working in batches, in a blender or the bowl of a food processor fitted with the steel blade, puree the tomato mixture until smooth, about 3 minutes. (As you blend the tomato mixture, you can gradually increase the speed as it begins to thin into a puree.) Return the puree to the saucepan. (Alternatively, puree the tomato mixture directly in the saucepan using an immersion blender).

5. Bring the puree to a simmer over medium-low heat. Meanwhile, in a small bowl or glass measuring cup, combine the cornstarch with 1 tablespoon cold water and whisk to combine. Add the cornstarch slurry to the ketchup and cook, stirring, for 1 minute to thicken. Remove the ketchup from the heat and transfer to an airtight container. Let cool to room temperature. Stored in an airtight container in the refrigerator, the ketchup will keep for up to 10 days.

THE ART OF PICNICKING

When the days turn warm and it's a crime to be inside, Jackie and I grab the kids, picnic basket, and Dog and head outside. In Portland, we never know how long a lovely day will last, so we try to make the most of it. We even keep our picnic basket prestocked with a few staples so we don't lose a minute of sunshine searching for anything when it's time to pack it up. Along with plates, cups, and napkins, we typically have a small pepper grinder, a bottle of hot sauce, a vial of kosher salt, and a little container of chili flakes in our basket, just in case.

When I'm packing our picnic basket, I'm all about cold food. Cold picnic foods take my Missouri mind back to the long summer days of my childhood, and offer a simple approach to eating outdoors. You'll almost always find cold fried chicken, chilled deviled eggs, crisp pickles, and a big glass of something sweet in my basket. (I'm partial to the kind of sun tea my late aunt Ronda Salmons used to keep out in her yard during the hot Missouri summers.)

I like to dress things up a bit to add some style to the cool comfort and relaxed vibe that a picnic is all about. So I throw on something a little fancy, like my favorite seersucker shorts, and bring a cozy blanket or quilt that's been passed down through the family—the kind that makes you want to take a nap as soon as you lay down on it is best. I also bring a cornhole set to play and put some lawn chairs up so I can watch the day pass by with the clouds up above and good company all around. The only thing left to do is eat. Now that's my kind of afternoon. —AS

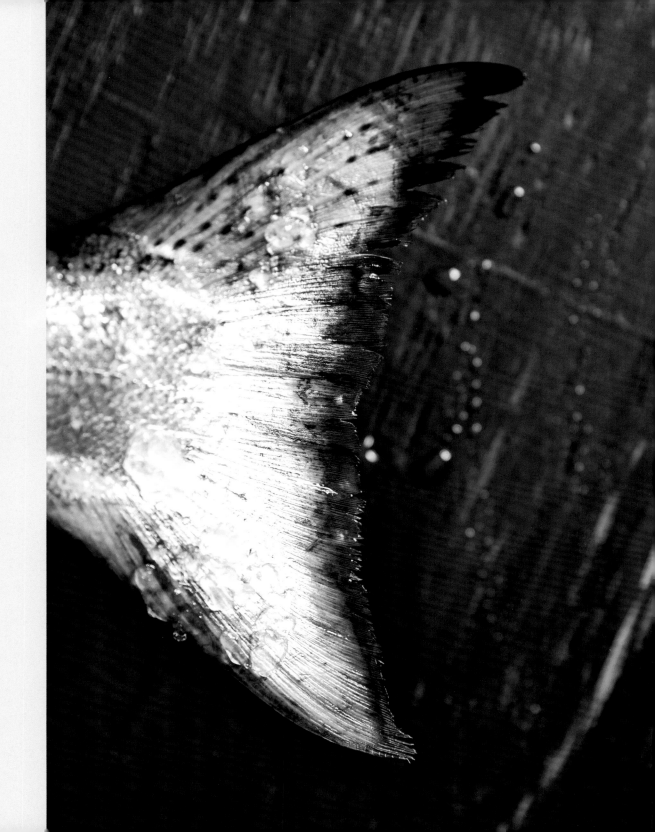

FINS AND SHELLS

Growing up in landlocked Missouri, the only fish I ever ate came from a lake or a river. We had crappie and blue gill, small flaky white fish; white bass, a firm white-fleshed fish; and catfish. They were all perfect for—you guessed it—frying. When I moved out to the Pacific Northwest and discovered salmon, steelhead, mussels, clams, oysters, crabs, and more, it was a revelation. I was so intrigued by all the seafood and the techniques I could apply to cook them that I had to try my hand at every one. From brining to roasting to grilling to poaching to frying, my favorite ways to prepare fish and shellfish today incorporate my American roots, as well as the roots I've put down in Oregon. —AS

Salt-Baked Steelhead with Soft Herbs, Lemon, and Cracked Fennel Seed

Serves 4

My boys and I like hearty foods, so when I make something light like this herb-crusted steelhead for family dinner, we call it "mama food" in honor of my lovely Jackie. Salt baking the steelhead is a technique I picked up early in my cooking career from my mentor at Wildwood, Cory Schreiber. In my opinion, it is the ultimate way to prepare the fish. While the steelhead bakes, the salt evens out the heat and locks the moisture inside the fish. I often make this dish when we are having company over because it is easy to double and tastes as good at room temperature as it does warm. Serve it with a side of Chanterelle and Blackberry Succotash (page 218), fresh peas tossed in butter, or a platter of roasted asparagus. —AS

1 cup rock salt or kosher salt

½ cup roughly chopped fresh flat-leaf parsley

1½ tablespoons fresh finely chopped tarragon

1½ tablespoons finely chopped fresh thyme

1 tablespoon cracked fennel seed
(see Chef's Note, page opposite)

1½ teaspoons lemon pepper

Finely grated zest of ½ lemon

Finely grated zest of ½ orange

1 (1½-pound) side of skin-on steelhead fillet

1½ tablespoons extra-virgin olive oil

Kosher salt, for seasoning

1. Arrange a rack in the center of the oven and preheat the oven to 325°F. Line a large baking sheet with parchment paper. Pour the rock salt on top of the parchment paper and spread it around with your hands to form an even layer. Set aside.

2. In a medium bowl, combine the parsley, tarragon, thyme, fennel seed, lemon pepper, lemon zest, and orange zest and mix until just combined. Set aside.

3. Place the steelhead, skin-side down, on top of the salt on the baking sheet. Using your hands, massage the oil into the flesh until it is evenly distributed. Season the steelhead with kosher salt, then gently press the herb mixture onto the flesh to cover the fillet evenly.

4. Bake the steelhead for 20 minutes or until the flesh is just opaque in the center. Transfer the steelhead to a large serving platter and serve family-style, or divide it into four portions and transfer to individual serving plates. Dig in immediately or wait to serve at room temperature.

Chef's Note: To crack fennel seed, place the desired amount in a mortar and pestle and pound until they are cracked into small pieces but not finely ground.

Bacon-Wrapped Trout with Summer Vegetables

Serves 4

River-run or brook-run fish like trout often need a little help in the flavor department. Spreading a bit of herbed butter inside a whole fish and wrapping it in bacon does the trick and is a foolproof way to keep the flesh moist. It also turns trout into an aesthetically pleasing dish you can serve to company over a bed of colorful summer vegetables. —AS

Bacon-Wrapped Trout

6 tablespoons (¾ stick) unsalted butter, at room temperature

4 tablespoons extra-virgin olive oil

1 tablespoon lemon pepper

1 tablespoon kosher salt

1 tablespoon finely chopped fresh thyme

4 (8- to 10-ounce) whole head-on trout, pin bones and fins removed

20 thin bacon slices (about 1 pound)

Summer Vegetables

1 tablespoon unsalted butter

1 tablespoon extra-virgin olive oil

2 small yellow crookneck squash, cut into ½-inch rounds

2 small zucchini, cut into ½-inch rounds

Kosher salt

2 medium ears corn, cut into ½-inch rounds

2 small red onions, quartered

¼ pound green beans, trimmed and blanched

2 garlic cloves, finely chopped

1 pint cherry tomatoes, halved

2 tablespoons finely chopped fresh oregano

2 tablespoons finely chopped fresh thyme

Finely grated zest and freshly squeezed juice of 1 lemon, plus more lemon juice for seasoning

continued on page 138

1. **Make the bacon-wrapped trout:** Arrange a rack in the center of the oven and preheat the oven to 350°F.

2. In a small bowl, combine 4 tablespoons of the butter, 2 tablespoons of the oil, lemon pepper, salt, and thyme and mix with a rubber spatula to combine. Set aside.

3. Working with one trout at a time, rinse the trout under cool running water for about 10 seconds per side to thoroughly clean the skin. Place the rinsed trout on a dry kitchen towel and pat dry. (The trout has to be completely dry before you start cooking.) Set aside.

4. Arrange four 18 by 13-inch pieces of parchment paper on your counter. Working with one sheet at a time, with the longest edge parallel to you, arrange 5 slices of bacon on the parchment paper, overlapping slightly and parallel to you. (It should look as if you are making a bacon blanket for the trout.) Place the trout on top of the bacon, perpendicular to you, about ¼ inch from the edge of the parchment paper. Open the trout like a book and, using a small rubber spatula, spread about 1 tablespoon of the herb butter on the inside of the trout. Fold the trout closed like a book. Using both hands, lift the parchment paper up and over the trout to drape the bacon over the top. Using a pulling motion, tuck the bacon under the belly side of the trout and gently roll it to the ends of the bacon slices. Repeat with the remaining bacon and trout and set aside.

5. In a 12-inch cast-iron skillet set over medium-high heat, warm 1 tablespoon of the butter and 1 tablespoon of the oil until they are combined and reach a hot, wavy state.

In a second 12-inch cast-iron skillet set over medium-high heat, warm the remaining 1 tablespoon olive oil and remaining 1 tablespoon butter until they are combined and reach a hot, wavy state. Place two of the bacon-wrapped trout in each skillet and cook until the bacon is lightly caramelized, about 3 minutes. Gently flip the trout over and cook on the second side until the bacon is lightly caramelized, about 2 minutes more. Drain the fat from the skillets and transfer the skillets to the oven to cook for 7 minutes or until the bacon is crisp and the trout is cooked through.

6. **Meawhile, make the summer vegetables:** In a large lidded skillet or saucepan set over medium-high heat, warm the butter and oil until the butter has melted and is hot but not browned. Add the squash and zucchini, season with salt, and toss to combine. Cook, stirring occasionally, until the vegetables are lightly caramelized, about 2 minutes. Add the corn, onions, green beans, and garlic and toss to combine. Cover, reduce the heat to medium, and cook, stirring occasionally, until the vegetables are lightly caramelized and start to release some liquid, about 5 minutes more. Add the cherry tomatoes, oregano, thyme, lemon zest, and lemon juice, remove the skillet from the heat, and toss together. Season with salt and additional lemon juice.

7. Spoon the vegetables into the center of four large plates. Using a fish spatula, transfer the trout from the skillets and place one trout on each plate, directly on top of the vegetables. Now eat.

Peel 'n' Eat Shrimp

Serves 4 to 6

My mom can't cook shrimp to save her life. (Sorry, Nance!) So when I started cooking professionally, I set out to create a peel 'n' eat shrimp recipe that even she could make. Instead of cooking the shrimp on the stovetop, I make a homemade court bouillon, pour the warm liquid over the raw shrimp, and let them sit and absorb its flavors. In about six minutes, you'll have perfectly cooked shrimp that are tasty enough to serve with just a squeeze of fresh lemon juice, but are even better dipped in creamy Homemade Tartar Sauce (page 151).

If you use frozen shrimp in this recipe, make sure they are fully thawed before pouring the bouillon over the top. —AS

2 tablespoons whole black peppercorns

2 tablespoons celery seed

2 tablespoons ground coriander

2 tablespoons ground fennel seed

2 tablespoons lemon pepper

2 tablespoons yellow mustard seed

¼ cup dry white wine, such as Chardonnay

2 tablespoons garlic powder

2 tablespoons sweet paprika

2 tablespoons kosher salt

Finely grated zest and freshly squeezed juice of 1 lemon

Finely grated zest and freshly squeezed juice of 1 orange

3 pounds (16/20 count) fresh or frozen shell-on deveined shrimp

Lemon wedges, for serving

1. In a large pot, combine the peppercorns, celery seed, coriander, fennel seed, lemon pepper, and mustard seed and cook over medium heat, stirring continuously, until the spices are toasted and fragrant, about 5 minutes. Add the wine and cook, scraping any fond from the bottom of the pot. Add the garlic powder, paprika, salt, lemon zest, lemon juice, orange zest, and orange juice and stir to combine. Add 1 gallon water, raise the heat to medium-high, and bring the court bouillon to a rolling boil.

2. Place the shrimp in a large bowl or container large enough to hold the shrimp and bouillon. Pour the bouillon through a strainer over the shrimp. (If necessary, you can divide the shrimp and bouillon between two containers.) Discard the spices in the strainer. Let stand until the shrimp are pink throughout, 8 to 10 minutes.

3. Carefully remove the shrimp from the bouillon and transfer them to a large platter. Discard the bouillon. Dig in immediately, with lemon wedges on the side.

Razor Clams "Rockefeller"

Serves 4

I've always considered the baked oyster dish known as oysters Rockefeller to be a true American dish and one worthy of serving at special occasions. When I moved to Oregon, I decided to create a Rockefeller-inspired starter using local razor clams in place of the oysters. Since it's hard to buy razor clams in their shells, I bake the shelled clams in ramekins with the bread crumb mixture on top. If you can't get razor clams, you could make this dish with a similarly large, long-shelled clam like the Ipswich clams you can find on the East Coast. —AS

1 tablespoon unsalted butter

¼ cup plus 1 tablespoon extra-virgin olive oil

1 cup homemade bread crumbs

2 tablespoons finely chopped fresh flat-leaf parsley

Kosher salt and freshly ground black pepper

Nonstick cooking spray

1 pound razor clam meat, cut into ¼-inch strips

6 garlic cloves, finely chopped

2 small shallots, finely chopped

1 to 1½ teaspoons chili flakes

Finely grated zest of 2 lemons

2 cups packed baby spinach leaves

1. In a medium skillet set over medium heat, combine the butter with 1 tablespoon of the oil and warm until the butter melts. Add the bread crumbs and cook, stirring occasionally, until toasted, about 3 minutes. Remove the skillet from the heat, stir in the parsley, and season with salt and pepper. Set aside.

2. Arrange a rack in the center of the oven and preheat the oven to 350°F. Coat four 6-ounce ramekins with nonstick cooking spray and set aside.

3. In a large skillet set over medium-high heat, warm the remaining ¼ cup olive oil until very hot. Remove the skillet from the heat and immediately add the razor clams. Add the garlic, shallots, chili flakes, and lemon zest and stir to combine.

4. Return the skillet to high heat and cook the clams, stirring continuously, until they start to curl and shrink, about 30 seconds. Add the spinach and cook, stirring continuously, until the spinach wilts, about 2 minutes. Season with salt and pepper.

5. Divide the razor clam mixture among the prepared ramekins, filling each nearly full. Top each serving with 2 tablespoons of the bread crumb and parsley mixture. Bake until the clams are tender, about 7 minutes. Remove the ramekins from the oven and dig in.

Manila Clams with Country Ham, Peas, and Mint

Serves 4 to 6

There's nothing like the sight of a pot of steaming clams. I combine them with salty country ham, sweet English peas, herbaceous mint, and mild spring onions in this zesty springtime dish. Farmers harvest spring onions before the bulbs grow to full size; they have small white or deep purple bulbs and tall green tops. (Use two sweet onions here if you can't find spring onions at a farmers' market or upscale grocer.) Buy your clams fresh from a tank; they should be clean and smell like the ocean. —AS

3 tablespoons bacon fat or unsalted butter

1 pound country ham, cut into ½-inch cubes

12 garlic cloves, thinly sliced

5 medium spring onions, trimmed and thinly sliced

2 teaspoons kosher salt

1¾ cups dry white wine, such as Chardonnay

Finely grated zest and freshly squeezed juice of 2 lemons

½ teaspoon freshly ground black pepper

5 pounds Manila clams, scrubbed

¾ cup heavy cream

½ pound fresh or frozen shelled English peas

⅓ cup torn fresh mint leaves

2 tablespoons finely chopped fresh flat-leaf parsley

1. In a large stockpot set over medium heat, warm the bacon fat or the butter until it melts. Add the ham and cook, stirring occasionally, until crisp, about 8 minutes. Add the garlic, spring onions, and salt and stir to combine. Cover and cook, stirring occasionally, until softened, about 3 minutes.

2. Add the wine, lemon zest, lemon juice, and pepper and stir to combine. Bring the mixture to a simmer. Add the clams and stir to combine. Cover and cook for 6 minutes, stirring halfway through to encourage the clams to open. Add the cream, cover, and cook the clams, stirring halfway through, until they open, about 6 minutes more.

3. Turn off the heat and add the peas, mint, and parsley to the pot. Cover and let sit for 2 minutes. Ladle large scoops of the clams, ham, peas, and broth into four to six large shallow bowls and serve hot.

Crispy Fried Oysters with Smoky Bacon and Green Apple Ragout

Serves 4

It might seem unusual, but I've always found green apple to be a great addition to creamy seafood dishes like clam chowder and this stew. The naturally acidic fruit adds a bright, clean flavor to the ragout and plays really well with the brininess of the fried oysters I serve on top. If you can't find fresh oysters, you can use jarred oysters in their place. —AS

Smoky Bacon and Green Apple Ragout

2 tablespoons unsalted butter

6 thick-cut bacon slices, cut into thirds

1 medium yellow onion, finely chopped

1 medium fennel bulb, finely chopped

3 medium celery stalks, peeled, trimmed and finely chopped (see Chef's Note, page 93)

1 Granny Smith apple, cored and finely chopped

1 cup unsweetened apple cider

2 tablespoons finely chopped fresh sage leaves

2 tablespoons finely chopped fresh thyme

1 cup heavy cream

Finely grated zest and freshly squeezed juice of 1 lemon

Kosher salt and freshly ground black pepper

Fried Oysters

2 cups vegetable oil, for frying

1 cup all-purpose flour

1 cup finely ground cornmeal

2 tablespoons lemon pepper

1 tablespoon garlic powder

1 tablespoon onion powder

1 tablespoon kosher salt

2 teaspoons ground celery seed

2 teaspoons freshly ground black pepper

12 fresh extra-small oysters, such as Willapa Bay oysters, shucked

2 tablespoons finely chopped fresh flat-leaf parsley, for garnish

1. **Make the smoky bacon and green apple ragout:** In a 12-inch skillet set over medium heat, warm the butter until it melts. Add the bacon and cook, stirring occasionally, until crisp, about 5 minutes. Drain off half the fat from the skillet. Add the onion, fennel, and celery and cook, stirring occasionally, until translucent, about 5 minutes. Add the apple and cook, stirring occasionally, until the apple starts to soften and incorporate into the vegetable mixture, about 5 minutes more.

2. Add the apple cider, sage, and thyme and cook, stirring occasionally, until the mixture has thickened like a ragout and the liquid has reduced by about half, about 5 minutes. Add the cream and cook until it has reduced enough to coat the back of a spoon, about 3 minutes. (At this point, the ragout should be thick and stewy.) Add the lemon zest and lemon juice. Season with salt and pepper. Remove the skillet from the heat and cover to keep warm.

3. **Make the fried oysters:** Line a baking sheet with paper towels. In a 12-inch cast-iron skillet set over medium heat, warm the oil until it reaches 350°F on a deep-frying thermometer.

4. In a medium bowl, combine the flour, cornmeal, lemon pepper, garlic powder, onion powder, salt, celery seed, and black pepper and whisk to combine.

5. Working in two batches, toss the oysters in the seasoned flour, then place in the hot oil and fry until crispy and golden brown, turning halfway through, about 5 minutes. Using a slotted spoon, transfer the oysters to the paper towel–lined baking sheet. Repeat with the remaining oysters.

6. Divide the ragout among four soup bowls. Divide the oysters among the bowls, placing them on top of the ragout in each bowl. Garnish with the parsley and dig in.

Boiled Crab with Scampi Butter

Serves 4 (makes about 1¼ cups scampi butter)

Dungeness crab is like the lobster of the West Coast. If you're serving it, you can bet there's a special occasion involved. You can make life easy and buy precooked crabs, but I'm going to suggest that you buy—or even catch—live crabs and cook them yourself. It's the freshest way to eat them, and cooking the crabs really enhances the experience. You'll have a greater respect for the animal when you start with a live one and cook it yourself.

When I make boiled crab at home, I put out plenty of cracking utensils and cover our table in large pieces of newspaper to make cleanup easy. You can serve the crab with sides of boiled potatoes, Caesar salad, and crusty bread, and offer guests plenty of scampi butter for dipping. If you find yourself with extra scampi butter, refrigerate it to use another day. It keeps for up to 3 days and is as great on pasta and chicken as it is with boiled crab. —AS

Boiled Crab

2 cups kosher salt

2 (2- to 3-pound) live Dungeness crabs

Scampi Butter

8 tablespoons (1 stick) unsalted butter, cut into ½-inch cubes

½ cup dry white wine, such as Chardonnay

4 garlic cloves, thinly sliced

1 small shallot, finely chopped

1¾ teaspoons kosher salt, plus more for seasoning

1½ teaspoons Worcestershire sauce

1 teaspoon freshly ground black pepper, plus more for seasoning

Finely grated zest of 2 lemons

Freshly squeezed juice of 1 lemon, plus more for seasoning

12 dashes Tabasco sauce

2 tablespoons roughly chopped fresh flat-leaf parsley

1. **Make the boiled crab:** In a 5-gallon stockpot, combine the salt with 3 gallons water. (The water should taste like the ocean.) Bring the water to a simmer over high heat. Using tongs, add the crabs to the pot, cover, and bring the water back up to a simmer. Once the water is at a simmer, turn the heat off and let the crabs sit in the water for 25 minutes.

2. **Meanwhile, make the scampi butter:** In a small saucepan set over medium heat, warm the butter until it melts. Add the wine, garlic, shallot, salt, Worcestershire, pepper, lemon zest, lemon juice, and Tabasco and stir to combine. Bring the mixture to a light simmer. Remove the saucepan from the heat and stir in the parsley. Season with salt, pepper, and additional lemon juice and cover to keep warm.

3. Transfer the crabs from the stockpot to a cutting board. Pull the claws off the crabs, split the bodies in half, and remove the top shells. Gently rinse the crab pieces under cold water to remove any impurities and transfer the bodies and claws to a large serving platter. Transfer the scampi butter to small ramekins to pass on the side for easy dipping. Dig in.

Heartland Fish Fry with Homemade Tartar Sauce, page 150

Heartland Fish Fry with Homemade Tartar Sauce

Serves 4

The first key to success for a good fish fry is to invite friends and family who aren't shy about having fun and eating a ton. Have the fish fry when the weather is nice so you can do your frying outside. If you haven't spent the day fishing, go buy nice fresh white fish like halibut, cod, catfish, rockfish, or trout from a good fish market or grocery store. Serve the crispy fish with a buffet of fresh salads, slaw, and plenty of homemade tartar sauce for dipping. —AS

6 medium fresh white fish fillets (about 1½ pounds), such as rockfish, halved and pin bones removed

1¼ cups low-fat buttermilk

1 cup all-purpose flour

1 cup finely ground cornmeal

1 tablespoon ground celery seed

1 tablespoon ground fennel seed

1 tablespoon garlic powder

1 tablespoon lemon pepper

2 teaspoons onion powder

2 teaspoons kosher salt

2 teaspoons freshly ground black pepper

2 cups lard or vegetable oil, for frying

Homemade Tartar Sauce (page opposite), for serving

1. In a large bowl, combine the fish with the buttermilk and, using your hands or a rubber spatula, move the fish around so the fillets are submerged. Cover the bowl with plastic wrap and let the fish soak in the refrigerator for 1 hour.

2. Line a large baking sheet with parchment paper. In a large bowl, combine the flour, cornmeal, celery seed, fennel seed, garlic powder, lemon pepper, onion powder, salt, and black pepper and whisk to combine. Working with one piece at a time, remove the fish from the buttermilk, allowing any excess buttermilk to drip back into the bowl. Place the fillet in the seasoned flour, shake the bowl to cover, and press down firmly to coat. Shake the fillet to remove any excess flour and place it on the prepared baking sheet. Repeat with the remaining fillets.

3. Line a large baking sheet with paper towels. In a large cast-iron skillet set over medium heat, warm the lard until it reaches 325°F on a deep-frying thermometer. Working in batches, fry the fillets, turning with a fish fork halfway through, until golden brown on the outside and snow white and cooked through in the center, about 3 minutes per side.

4. Transfer the fish to the paper towel–lined baking sheet to drain. Repeat with the remaining fillets, then transfer the fried fish to a platter and serve up with tartar sauce alongside.

Homemade Tartar Sauce

Makes about 2½ cups

No fish fry is complete without a bowl of punchy tartar sauce. When you make your own from scratch, you can personalize it to suit your taste; I like to stir chopped capers and cornichons into mine and add Tabasco sauce for a little heat. Serve the sauce with fried fish or as a dip for French fries or Crispy Onion Rings (page 126). —AS

2 cups mayonnaise

1 medium shallot, finely chopped

2 tablespoons finely chopped fresh flat-leaf parsley

1 tablespoon capers, rinsed and roughly chopped

3 cornichons, roughly chopped

Finely grated zest and freshly squeezed juice of 1 lemon, plus more juice for seasoning

10 dashes Tabasco sauce, plus more for seasoning

Kosher salt

1. In a small bowl, combine the mayonnaise, shallot, parsley, capers, cornichons, lemon zest, lemon juice, and Tabasco and use a rubber spatula or large spoon to combine. Season with salt and additional lemon juice and Tabasco.

2. Transfer the tartar sauce to the refrigerator to chill for 30 minutes before serving. Stored in an airtight container in the refrigerator, the tartar sauce will keep for up to 3 days.

FRIDAY NIGHT FISH FRY

A special sense of excitement comes over me when I hear the words "fish fry." A Midwest fish fry with my mom's side of the family, the Gaineses, was and still is a special treat. My uncles Tim and Greg and their dad, Grampa Jack, go down to the Lake of the Ozarks and catch as many crappie and blue gill as they can. As they finish loading up their spoils, they ring the telephone beacon. It's the cattle call that lets the family know it's time to gather on Mom's back porch and get busy with some serious frying.

The first task at hand is to clean the flaky little fish. Then out come the Fry Daddies, the cornmeal mix, and plenty of cold, frosty beverages. Tim and Greg man the fryers, and the brotherly banter between the two of them is almost as good as the fish they are frying. At their sides, platters covered with wadded-up paper towels soak up the extra fat as the pieces of fish come out of the fryers and pile up to the heights of a great pyramid. Anticipation begins to get the best of everyone as the family starts to zero in on that one piece that's gonna start it all for them. When the platters are full and the uncles give the thumbs-up to dig in, the frenzy begins.

We fill our plates with those crispy, flaky morsels of heaven along with sides of creamy potato salad, coleslaw, cornbread, and sliced tomatoes. As people pile mounds of fish on their plates, they give little thought that their eyes may be bigger than their stomachs. The room gets quiet as we stuff ourselves like it's the last fish fry of our life. We can't help but be tempted by the smell of the hot grease hitting the cornmeal mix and by that last helping of Mom's coleslaw that pushes us over the edge. —AS

THE BIRDS

I'll occasionally throw a whole chicken in the oven to roast, but, more times than not, I find that breaking down a bird and treating each piece with a different cooking method brings out the best flavor. The breast cooks differently from the thigh, which is different from the leg, which is different from the tail, and so on. This is especially true for the Thanksgiving turkey. We have all seen the Norman Rockwell painting of the family gathered at the table with the beautifully roasted turkey as the centerpiece. It sure looks good, but how did it taste? In this chapter, I'll show you a better way to prepare the birds as I get busy cooking everything from braised duck legs to the granddaddy of them all, the Thanksgiving turkey. —AS

Skillet-Fried Chicken

Serves 4 to 6

My granny Cris had a long history with fried chicken. When she was a little girl back in the early 1900s, she delivered the crispy bird to the inmates at the old Maries County Jail, passing it through a little window right into their cells. As an adult, she made it often, and there was nothing that woman cooked better. She took the time to shake each piece in a brown paper bag, then fried it in lard in her soulful cast-iron skillet. It was the real deal, and the defining dish of my Midwest childhood.

When we opened The Cat, I knew fried chicken would be our signature dish. There's simply no substitute for good fried chicken, and I've upped my game by brining it in salt water for a day and soaking it in buttermilk for another day. Then I shake the chicken in a well-seasoned flour (my secret ingredient is lemon pepper) and fry it in beef suet. (You can use lard at home if you can't get beef suet from your butcher.) And just like my granny did, I always make my fried chicken in a cast-iron skillet. If you make it in anything else, the soul of the dish disappears. —AS

¼ cup kosher salt

2 each skin-on boneless chicken breasts, thighs, drumettes, and wings, breasts halved (see Chef's Note)

4 cups low-fat buttermilk

3⅓ cups all-purpose flour

⅓ cup lemon pepper

¼ cup garlic powder

¼ cup ground celery seed

2 tablespoons onion powder

4 cups beef tallow or lard

1. One to 2 days before serving the chicken, in a large pitcher, mix 2 quarts water with 2 tablespoons of the salt and stir until the salt has dissolved. Place the chicken in a large bowl and pour the salt water over the top to cover it completely. Cover the bowl with plastic wrap and let the chicken soak in the refrigerator for at least 12 hours or up to 24 hours.

2. Remove the chicken from the salt water and discard the water. Rinse the bowl and return the chicken to it. Pour the buttermilk over the chicken to cover it completely. Cover the bowl with plastic wrap and let the chicken soak in the refrigerator for at least 12 hours or up to 24 hours.

continued on page 158

3. When the chicken is ready, line a large baking sheet with parchment paper. In a large paper grocery bag, combine the flour, lemon pepper, garlic powder, celery seed, onion powder, and remaining 2 tablespoons salt and shake the bag until combined. Working with one piece at a time, remove the chicken from the buttermilk, allowing any excess buttermilk to drip back into the bowl. Place the chicken in the seasoned flour and shake the bag until the chicken is well coated. Place the chicken on the prepared baking sheet and repeat with the remaining pieces of chicken. Transfer the baking sheet to the refrigerator and allow the dredged chicken to rest for at least 30 minutes or up to 1 hour.

4. Line a separate large baking sheet with paper towels. In a 12-inch cast-iron skillet set over medium heat, warm the beef tallow or lard until it reaches 325°F on a deep-frying thermometer. Place five pieces of chicken in the skillet and fry, turning with a fish fork every 5 minutes and adjusting the heat to maintain a steady temperature, until the skin is golden brown and the chicken is cooked through, about 15 minutes for the breasts, legs, and thighs, and about 10 minutes for the wings. (To check the chicken for doneness, remove a piece from the skillet and insert two of the prongs from your fish fork into the thickest part of the chicken flesh. The juices should run clear and warm.)

5. Transfer the fried chicken to the paper towel–lined baking sheet to drain. Fry the remaining chicken, then transfer the chicken to a platter and dig in.

Chef's Note: I use boneless skin-on chicken meat to make fried chicken easy for everyone to eat—and I encourage everyone to eat fried chicken with their fingers. If you want to go the boneless route, just ask your butcher to debone a 4-pound chicken, cut it into ten pieces, and leave the skin intact. If you use bone-in pieces instead, you may need to fry them for a few minutes longer.

"Sappy Spice" Grilled Chicken

Serves 4 to 6

This savory spice rub is my signature blend when I'm grilling chicken. (I use it so often Jackie named it after me.) We make this main course often in the summertime because it's a nice light dish that's great served with summer salads like Melon Salad with Arugula, Fennel, and Marjoram (page 82) or Grilled Corn Salad with Bing Cherries and Goat Cheese (page 76) on the side. —AS

2 tablespoons lemon pepper

1 tablespoon ground fennel seed

1 tablespoon garlic powder

1 tablespoon herbes de Provence (without lavender)

1 tablespoon sweet paprika

1 (5-pound) chicken, cut into 8 pieces

Kosher salt

1. In a small bowl, combine the lemon pepper, fennel seed, garlic powder, herbes de Provence, and paprika and whisk to combine. Set aside.

2. Arrange the chicken in a large glass baking pan or on a large baking sheet and season with salt. Sprinkle the spice mixture evenly and liberally over all the sides of the chicken pieces. Cover the chicken with plastic wrap and refrigerate for 2 hours.

3. Prepare a fire in a charcoal grill and let it burn down to glowing coals. Spread the coals evenly on the base and place the grill grate 6 inches above the coals. When the grill is hot, place the chicken on the grill over direct heat, skin-side up, and cover the grill. Grill the chicken until caramelized on the bottom, about 20 minutes.

4. Using a pair of tongs, flip the chicken over and grill, skin-side down, until the skin is crisp and caramelized, about 20 minutes more or until you can poke it with a fish fork and the juices run clear. (Play close attention to the chicken at this point to control flare-ups in the barbecue from the fat dripping onto the coals.) Transfer the chicken to a large platter and let rest for 5 minutes. Dig in.

Chef's Note: If you want to roast this chicken in the oven, follow the recipe through step 2, then arrange a rack in the center of the oven and preheat the oven to 375°F. Line a large baking sheet with parchment paper and place a rack on top. Arrange the chicken pieces on top of the rack and roast, turning the chicken halfway through, for about 40 minutes or until the skin is caramelized and the juices run clear. Let the chicken rest for 5 minutes. Dig in.

Brick-Pressed Cornish Game Hen with Grated Tomato Vinaigrette

Serves 4 (makes about 2 cups vinaigrette)

Late in the summer when you've grilled chicken until you're blue in the face, pick up some Cornish game hen. Its texture is similar to that of chicken but Cornish game hen has darker, richer meat and a sweeter taste. It's also a smaller bird, making it a nice size to serve for an intimate gathering with this fresh, full-bodied tomato vinaigrette. (Part of the appeal of the vinaigrette is the broken appearance that lets you see all the oil, pulp, thyme, and vinegar mingling in the bowl and eventually on the plate.)

Using a brick to put pressure on the hen on the grill is an age-old cooking method that keeps the bird flat while it cooks, ensures even cooking, and results in crispy, charred skin. This dish is a sure hit at any summer party.

Cornish game hens are often found in the freezer section of meat departments, so plan ahead to give them time to thaw. Then use kitchen shears to remove the backbone before marinating and grilling them. —AS

Brick-Pressed Cornish Game Hens

2 tablespoons extra-virgin olive oil

2 tablespoons finely chopped fresh rosemary

2 tablespoons finely chopped fresh thyme

1 tablespoon finely chopped fresh sage leaves

1 tablespoon kosher salt

Finely grated zest of 2 lemons

2 Cornish game hens, backbones removed

Grated Tomato Vinaigrette

3 ripe medium beefsteak tomatoes, halved along the equator

3 tablespoons extra-virgin olive oil

2 tablespoons red wine vinegar

2 teaspoons kosher salt, plus more for seasoning

1 teaspoon smoked paprika

1 teaspoon freshly ground black pepper, plus more for seasoning

1 teaspoon finely chopped fresh thyme

Finely grated zest of ½ orange

Freshly squeezed juice of 1 orange

1. **Make the brick-pressed Cornish game hens:** In a small bowl, combine the oil, rosemary, thyme, sage, salt, and lemon zest and mix to combine. Arrange the Cornish game hens on a small baking sheet and massage the herb mixture into the flesh and bone side of each hen. Transfer to the refrigerator to rest for 1 hour.

2. **Make the grated tomato vinaigrette:** With a large-toothed hand grater, grate the tomatoes into a medium nonreactive bowl, discarding the skins. (This pulp will provide the body, flavor, and texture for the vinaigrette.) Add the oil, vinegar, salt, paprika, pepper, thyme, orange zest, and orange juice to the pulp and stir with a large spoon to form a broken vinaigrette. Season with salt and pepper and set aside.

3. Prepare a fire in a charcoal grill and let it burn down to glowing coals. Wrap two large bricks tightly in aluminum foil. Spread the coals into a circle around the edge of the grill to create a halo for the hens and place the grill grate 6 inches above the coals. When the grill is hot, place the hens on the grill over indirect heat, bone-side down. Place a brick on top of each hen, cover the grill, and cook until the flesh starts to caramelize, about 10 minutes. (Keep an eye on the fire to ensure you don't get flare-ups from the fat dripping onto the coals.) Flip the hens, replace the bricks, and cook until the skin starts to caramelize, about 10 minutes more.

4. Flip the hens back over to the bone side and remove the bricks. Cook until the juices run clear in the thigh and leg and the skin is set and caramelized, about 5 minutes more. Remove the hens from the grill and let rest on a cutting board for 5 minutes. Using a sharp knife, cut each hen in half along the breastbone and set aside.

5. Spoon a pool of the vinaigrette into the middle of each of four dinner plates. (Reserve any remaining vinaigrette for another use. Stored in an airtight container in the refrigerator, it will keep for up to 3 days.) Place half of a hen on top of the vinaigrette on each plate and dig in.

Crispy Turkey Tails with Buttermilk Blue Cheese Dressing

Serves 4 to 6

A few years ago, I was shooting the shit with some chef friends in Austin, Texas, when someone mentioned they'd been eating a lot of turkey tails. I liked the idea of offering a different take on turkey that fit our whole-animal approach to cooking, so I got my hands on some tails and tried confiting them in duck fat. Now I serve the succulent cut often, with blue cheese dressing on the side.

You can get turkey tails in any season, but you'll probably need to special order them from a butcher. If you can't get your hands on duck fat, you can use lard or beef fat to confit the turkey tails instead. Just make sure you follow the instructions to confit the tails carefully. Hot duck fat can give you a nasty burn. —AS

1 teaspoon freshly ground black pepper

1 teaspoon ground coriander

1 teaspoon ground fennel seed

1 teaspoon kosher salt

1 teaspoon chili flakes

8 turkey tails

2 quarts rendered duck fat

Buttermilk Blue Cheese Dressing (opposite), for serving

1. In a medium bowl, combine the pepper, coriander, fennel seed, salt, and chili flakes and whisk to combine. Add the turkey tails to the bowl and toss with your hands to combine. Set aside and let rest at room temperature for at least 1 hour or cover with plastic wrap and refrigerate for up to 24 hours. (As the turkey tails rest, the seasoning will penetrate the flesh and the turkey tails will smell really sweet and spicy and look a little moist.)

2. Arrange a rack in the center of the oven and preheat the oven to 300°F. Meanwhile, transfer the turkey tails to a 9 by 13-inch baking pan and place the baking pan on a large rimmed baking sheet. Set aside.

3. In a medium saucepan set over low heat, warm the duck fat until it melts. Pouring from the edge of the baking pan, slowly pour the duck fat over the turkey tails to completely submerge them in the fat. Cover the baking pan with aluminum foil and carefully slide the baking sheet into the oven. Cook the turkey tails for 2 hours 30 minutes or until fork-tender.

4. Remove the foil and raise the oven temperature to 375°F. Continue cooking the turkey tails until they are browned and crispy on the edges, about 5 minutes more.

5. Line a large baking sheet with paper towels. When the turkey tails are crispy, turn off the oven and slowly pull out the oven rack. Using a slotted spoon, transfer the turkey tails to the paper towel–lined baking sheet and set aside to drain for a few minutes. Slide the oven rack and baking pan full of duck fat back into the oven and let the duck fat cool to room temperature before discarding it or straining and saving it for another use.

6. Transfer the turkey tails to a serving plate and dig in with a bowl of the blue cheese dressing on the side.

Buttermilk Blue Cheese Dressing

Makes about 2¾ cups

If you're making this rich, gutsy blue cheese dressing as a dip for turkey tails (opposite), you'll have enough left over to serve throughout the week over grilled chicken, as a dip for crunchy raw vegetables, or as a dressing for a wedge salad. —AS

½ cup plus 2 tablespoons Buttermilk Blue cheese

2 tablespoons garlic powder

2 tablespoons dried thyme

1½ tablespoons onion powder

1 (16-ounce) container full-fat sour cream

½ cup low-fat buttermilk

Kosher salt and freshly ground black pepper

1. Fill a saucepan with 1 inch of water and bring to a boil. Set a medium heatproof bowl over the water, being sure the bottom of the bowl doesn't touch the water. Place the cheese in the bowl and stir frequently until it melts, about 3 minutes. Remove the bowl from the heat, add the garlic powder, thyme, and onion powder, and whisk to form a paste.

2. Add the sour cream and whisk to combine. Gradually whisk in the buttermilk to thin the dressing until it has the consistency of reduced cream. Season with salt and pepper. Dig in, or transfer to an airtight container and refrigerate for up to 1 week.

Braised Duck Legs

Serves 4

People seem to think duck is too fussy to make at home. That's because they haven't made this one-pot meal. To ensure the duck legs have crispy skin and tender flesh, I brown them on the stovetop before braising them with kale, onions, and dried sour cherries in the oven.

A few notes when you're working with duck: It's best to sear the flesh side of the hindquarters first so when you flip them over and sear the skin side, it will stretch over the flesh instead of retracting. Second, when you are checking the legs to see if they're done, take the end of the leg bone and twist it with your hand. The bone should easily turn and release from the socket in the thigh. This is the way I check all fowl—chicken, pheasant, duck, you name it. It's a foolproof old Gramma trick that works every time. —AS

4 bone-in duck hindquarters (thighs and legs)

2 tablespoons finely chopped fresh thyme

1 tablespoon kosher salt, plus more for seasoning

1½ teaspoons freshly ground black pepper, plus more for seasoning

2 tablespoons unsalted butter

1 large yellow onion, thinly sliced

3 garlic cloves, finely chopped

1 cup fruity red wine, such as Zinfandel

3 tablespoons balsamic vinegar

3 cups chicken stock

½ cup dried sour cherries

2 bunches lacinato kale, stems removed, leaves cut into ½-inch-wide strips

1. Lay the duck legs skin-side down on a large baking sheet. In a small bowl, combine the thyme with the salt and pepper and whisk to combine. Rub half of the spice mixture over the duck legs. Turn the duck legs over and apply the remaining rub to the skin side. Let the duck legs rest for 1 hour at room temperature or cover and refrigerate for up to 24 hours.

2. Arrange a rack in the center of the oven and preheat the oven to 375°F. Meanwhile, in a 12-inch cast-iron skillet set over medium-high heat, warm the butter until it melts. Add the duck legs, flesh-side down, and cook until golden brown, about 5 minutes. Turn the duck legs over and cook, skin-side down, until golden brown, about 5 minutes more. Transfer the duck legs to a large plate and set aside.

3. Leaving all the fat and fond in the skillet, add the onions and 2 tablespoons water and cook over medium heat, stirring occasionally, until caramelized, about 5 minutes. Add the garlic and cook, stirring occasionally, until fragrant and lightly browned, about 1 minute more.

4. Add the wine and vinegar to the skillet and continue cooking until the wine has reduced by half and the onion-garlic mixture looks stewlike, about 5 minutes. Add the stock and cherries and raise the heat to high. Bring the mixture to a simmer and add the kale. Cover and cook until the kale wilts, about 3 minutes.

5. Nestle the reserved duck legs, skin-side up, in the kale mixture. Transfer the skillet to the oven and braise the duck legs for 1 hour. Rotate the skillet from front to back and braise the duck legs for 30 minutes more or until the duck is tender, the skin is a nice amber color, and the braising liquid has reduced, leaving you with a stewlike mixture.

6. Remove the skillet from the oven and season the duck and kale-cherry mixture with salt and pepper. Using a slotted spoon, transfer the duck legs to a large serving platter or four individual serving plates. Scoop the kale-cherry mixture out of the skillet and place it on the side of the duck legs, making sure not to moisten the skin so it stays crisp. Dig in.

Braised Duck Legs, page 164

Brined and Smoked Thanksgiving Turkey, page 168

Brined and Smoked Thanksgiving Turkey

Serves 8

I'm proud to say that I've never cooked a turkey the traditional way in my entire life. Here's why: When you break down the whole bird into parts, you can cook each part in the most forgiving and painless way possible. Simply brine and smoke the breast and marinate and braise the legs, and boom—it's done! When it comes time to serve that bird, you'll be the hero who cooked a juicy, tender Thanksgiving turkey that everyone will talk about for years to come. I'll be damned if anyone cooks a whole turkey again after trying this process. —AS

1 (12- to 14-pound) turkey

4 cups packed light brown sugar

1½ cups kosher salt

½ cup ground fennel seed

¼ cup whole allspice berries

¼ cup whole black peppercorns

¼ cup juniper berries

5 star anise

Finely grated zest of 2 oranges

3 medium celery stalks, trimmed, peeled, and thinly sliced (see Chef's Note, page 93)

2 medium carrots, peeled, trimmed, and thinly sliced

2 medium yellow onions, thinly sliced

2 tablespoons finely chopped fresh rosemary

2 tablespoons finely chopped fresh thyme

1 tablespoon finely chopped fresh sage leaves

Kosher salt and freshly ground black pepper

2 cups hickory chips, for smoking

2 tablespoons vegetable oil

1 cup dry white wine, such as Chardonnay

2 quarts chicken stock

1. One day before serving, on a large cutting board, remove the legs and wings from the turkey, keeping both breasts intact and the spine attached, and set aside.

2. In a large pot, combine 2 quarts water, brown sugar, salt, fennel seed, allspice berries, peppercorns, juniper berries, star anise, and orange zest. Bring the mixture to a simmer over medium-high heat, stirring occasionally to help the sugar dissolve. Once the liquid is hot and the sugar has dissolved, remove the pot from the heat.

3. In a large stockpot or container, place 2 quarts ice cubes. Pour the brine over the ice cubes and stir to incorporate and cool down the brine. (The brine should feel lukewarm. If it is still hot, add a little more ice.) Place the turkey breasts in the brine, cover the container with a lid, aluminum foil, or plastic wrap, and refrigerate for 24 hours.

4. Meanwhile, in a large bowl, combine the celery, carrots, onions, rosemary, thyme, and sage. Season the turkey legs with salt and pepper. Add the turkey legs to the bowl and toss to combine. Cover the bowl with aluminum foil or plastic wrap and refrigerate overnight or up to 24 hours.

5. The next day, soak the wood chips according to the package instructions and preheat a smoker to 200°F. (Or see "Smoking Without a Smoker," page 35.) Remove the turkey breasts from the brine and pat dry. Place the wet hickory chips over the fire or in an electric hopper and smoke the turkey breast for 3 hours. Place a wire rack on a large baking sheet and transfer the turkey breasts to the wire rack to rest.

6. Meanwhile, arrange a rack in the center of the oven and preheat the oven to 350°F. Remove the turkey legs from the vegetables and set the vegetables aside. In a large Dutch oven set over medium heat, warm the oil. Place the turkey legs skin-side up in the pot and lightly brown them on all sides, about 5 minutes per side. Remove the turkey legs from the pot and set aside.

7. Add the vegetables to the pot and cook over medium-high heat, stirring occasionally, until slightly caramelized, about 10 minutes. Add the wine, scraping the bottom of the pot to incorporate the brown bits. Return the turkey legs to the pot, skin-side up, and add the stock. Bring the mixture to a simmer, then transfer the pot to the oven and braise the turkey legs for 2 hours or until they are fork-tender.

8. Remove the turkey legs from the oven and transfer them to a cutting board. Pull the meat off the legs, but don't shred it. Transfer the meat and vegetables to a large serving platter. Slice the turkey breasts and arrange the meat on the platter. Dig in.

COOKING WITH CAST IRON

A well-seasoned, well-used cast-iron skillet can bring a tear to my eye. They simply possess more soul. When I see one, I immediately think of old school American, grassroots cooking, and start jonesing to get into the kitchen. It's as if the skillet is singing an Etta James tune, and its siren song hypnotizes me to pick it up and get some music going in the pan.

A cast-iron skillet with some history is better than a new one you can buy at the store. You can pick up a pre-seasoned pan, but if you can score a worn-in skillet from a garage or estate sale, you've hit the jackpot. The skillet you're after should be shiny and black, not rusty, and should look like it's been used and well cared for. These winning pans have been seasoned by hand over time and give you the chance to bring a piece of another cook's culinary heritage into your home.

At home, I use the cast-iron skillet my stepdad, Mr. Marvin T. Jones, got as a wedding gift in 1958. He passed it on to me years ago, and I cook in it so often, it has become a fixture on our stove. I use it to make grilled cheese sandwiches, pancakes, and fried chicken, which has to be my favorite thing to cook in that pan.

There's no sense cooking fried chicken in anything other than a cast-iron skillet. The metal keeps the fat at the right temperature to provide a steady heat source and the consistency you need to guarantee even cooking. And when you use a cast-iron skillet, not a deep-fryer, to fry chicken, you have to tend the bird as it cooks. This way, you give the chicken the personal attention it deserves and get more authentic, more beautiful, evenly cooked fried chicken every time. —AS

My aunt Ronda used this cast-iron skillet to fry chicken by the ol' Gasconade River in Missouri.

Maries County Jail, where Maude Marie Murphy (aka Granny Cris) would deliver fried chicken to the inmates in the early 1900s.

Netarts Bay, Oregon, a hotbed for shellfish.

WHERE'S GRAMMA?

When my great-gramma Ruby Strong passed away back in the nineties, I inherited a lot of her old kitchen kink. There were old American cookbooks, pretty archaic and medieval-looking turn-of-the-century cookware, and the old carving fork that my great-grandpa Tom Crum Strong had made for Ruby by hand.

I fell in love with that old carving fork right away because it gave me an opportunity to bring Ruby with me into the kitchen. Naming the fork Gramma only seemed right.

Now, Gramma is a little squirrelly. In our small kitchen, she inevitably ends up sneaking away, or sometimes she falls or gets dropped in the heat of a rush and you'll catch me pacing around asking the other cooks, "Where's Gramma?" If she appears on someone else's cutting board, we say Gramma's two-timing me and I quickly snatch her up because I can't function on the line if I don't have her in my hand or at least in my sight.

Over the years, Gramma has become a grounding presence in my kitchen. I know I'll do things right if I have Gramma there, and I need her with me because she's the tool I use more than anything else. I grill with her, sauté with her, and use her to make fried chicken. No other tool can delicately flip, move, or scoop foods like Gramma does, and our cooks quickly learn about her versatility as they watch me cook. Then they go out to buy their own version of Gramma because they understand why she's so useful in the kitchen—and because I ain't sharing her. —AS

THE BUTCHER'S BLOCK

When it comes to cooking beef, pork, and lamb, I think of the whole beast. That's why I'm enamored with the art of butchery. Butchery to me isn't just about breaking down the whole animal into smaller pieces. It's a mental and physical approach to understanding how an animal moves through its life and how its muscle groups, organs, bones, blood, and tendons can be best prepared with proper cooking techniques. When you view an animal in this way, you become a more intuitive cook. Whether I'm using wet heat, dry heat, smoke, etc., the processes I use to cook various cuts play into my philosophy that every animal deserves to be treated with respect and care and that a chef should know what they want the end result to be on the plate before they make the first cut. The recipes that follow teach you how to look at pigs, cows, and lambs in a new way and how to cook my favorite cuts from each one. —AS

Chicken-Fried Steak with "Woo" Gravy

Serves 4

The first good chicken-fried steak I ever had was at Ron's Country Boy in Columbia, Missouri. I was hungover as shit. That big-ass steak hit the spot, and probably explains why I view chicken-fried steaks—or what I've come to think of as American schnitzel—as perfect brunch food. At The Cat, we slap our steaks on some mashed potatoes and slather 'em with "Woo"—or Worcestershire—Gravy. For a little color, cook up some greens to serve on the side. —AS

4 (6-ounce) top round steaks

2 cups low-fat buttermilk

3⅓ cups all-purpose flour

6 tablespoons lemon pepper

2 tablespoons garlic powder

2 tablespoons ground celery seed

2 tablespoons kosher salt

2 tablespoons onion powder

4 cups beef tallow or lard, for frying

"Woo" Gravy (opposite), for serving

Finely chopped fresh flat-leaf parsley, for garnish

1. Using a meat mallet or meat tenderizer, pound the steaks until they are ¼ inch thick. Put the steaks in a shallow roasting pan or large baking pan and pour the buttermilk over the top. Move the steaks around in the pan to ensure that the buttermilk coats all of the steaks. Cover the pan with plastic wrap and refrigerate for 30 minutes.

2. Line a large baking sheet with parchment paper and set aside. In a large bowl, combine the flour, lemon pepper, garlic powder, celery seed, salt, and onion powder and whisk to combine. Working with one steak at a time, place the steaks in the seasoned flour. Shake the bowl around and dredge the steaks, pressing the flour into the steaks to get an even coating. Place the steaks on the prepared baking sheet and let rest for 10 minutes.

3. Meanwhile, arrange a rack in the center of the oven and preheat the oven to 170°F. Line a separate large baking sheet with crumpled paper towels and set aside.

4. In a 12-inch cast-iron skillet set over medium-high heat, warm the beef tallow or lard until it reaches 350°F on a deep-frying thermometer. Working with one steak at a time, slowly lower the steak into the beef tallow, starting with the end closest to you and finishing with the end farthest away from you to prevent the beef tallow from splashing. Cook the steak for 3 minutes. Using a fish fork, turn the steak over and cook until crispy and golden brown on the second side, about 3 minutes more. Transfer the steak to the paper towel–lined baking sheet and keep warm in the oven while frying the remaining steaks.

5. Place one steak on each of four plates and spoon the gravy over the top. Garnish with the parsley and dig in.

"Woo" Gravy

Makes about 2 cups

My tangy Worcestershire gravy is made for serving with chicken-fried steaks. (We call it "Woo" Gravy because no one can ever spell or say Worcestershire right.) You can make it in advance and reheat it just before serving, or prepare it while the steaks are soaking in their buttermilk bath.

If you want to make the gravy in advance, let it cool to room temperature, cover, and refrigerate for up to 2 days. When ready to serve, transfer the gravy to a saucepan set over low heat and reheat, whisking frequently, until smooth and warmed through. —AS

½ cup rendered bacon fat

½ cup all-purpose flour

2 tablespoons packed light brown sugar

1½ teaspoons freshly ground black pepper, plus more for seasoning

1½ teaspoons kosher salt, plus more for seasoning

2 cups chicken stock

1 cup freshly brewed black coffee

½ cup Worcestershire sauce

1 tablespoon finely chopped fresh thyme

1. In a medium saucepan set over medium heat, warm the bacon fat until it melts. Add the flour and whisk to combine. Cook, whisking frequently, until the mixture darkens to the color of peanut butter, about 10 minutes. Add the sugar, pepper, and salt and whisk to combine.

2. Slowly whisk in the stock, coffee, and Worcestershire. Bring the mixture to a simmer, whisking occasionally, then add the thyme. Simmer, stirring occasionally, until the mixture thickens enough to coat the back of a spoon, about 20 minutes. Remove the gravy from the heat and season with salt and pepper.

Red Wine–Braised Beef with Wild Mushroom Steak Sauce

Serves 4 to 6

When it comes to beef, everyone praises steak, but this tender braised chuck roast is the epitome of the cow for me. From an early age, I saw how a big pot of braised beef encouraged families to sit down and share food in a way individual steaks never could. Think of this dish as an elevated pot roast. Serve it with the Wild Mushroom Steak Sauce, or surround it with seasonal sides like boiled or butter-braised potatoes in the winter, roasted asparagus in the spring, and fresh sliced tomatoes in the summer. —AS

Kosher salt

1 (2½- to 3-pound) boneless chuck roast

1 medium yellow onion, thinly sliced

1 medium fennel bulb, thinly sliced

8 garlic cloves, thinly sliced

1 tablespoon finely chopped fresh rosemary

3 tablespoons unsalted butter

1½ cups dry spicy red wine, such as Cabernet or Merlot

1 quart chicken or beef stock

Freshly ground black pepper

Wild Mushroom Steak Sauce (page 185), for serving

1. Liberally salt the chuck roast and set aside. In a medium bowl, combine the onion, fennel, garlic, and rosemary and toss to combine. Transfer half of the mixture to a large bowl and place the roast on top, then pack the remaining onion mixture over and around the roast. Cover the bowl with plastic wrap and refrigerate for at least 8 hours or overnight.

2. Arrange a rack in the center of the oven and preheat the oven to 350°F. Remove the roast from the refrigerator and set aside to come up to room temperature.

3. In a large Dutch oven set over medium heat, warm the butter until it melts. Remove the roast from the bowl, brushing any vegetables that cling to it back into the bowl. Set the vegetables aside. Put the roast in the pot and brown on all sides, about 4 minutes per side.

4. Transfer the roast to a plate or cutting board and add the reserved vegetables to the pot. Raise the heat to medium-high and cook, stirring occasionally, until the vegetables are caramelized, about 5 minutes. Add the wine, scraping the bottom of the pot with a wooden spoon

continued on page 184

to loosen all the brown bits. Bring the red wine to a simmer and simmer until it has reduced by half, about 5 minutes. Add the stock and bring to a simmer. Return the roast to the pot, cover, and transfer to the oven to braise for 2 hours 30 minutes or until fork-tender.

5. Remove the roast from the oven and let it rest for 10 minutes in the braising liquid. Season with pepper. Slice the roast directly in the pot, then transfer it to a large platter. (Discard the braising liquid and aromatics.) Spoon the wild mushroom sauce over the top and dig in.

Wild Mushroom Steak Sauce

Makes about 3 cups

Over the years, I've come up with a hundred different ways to serve braised beef; pairing it with this wild mushroom steak sauce is my favorite. The combination of meaty wild mushrooms and classic steakhouse flavors like Worcestershire sauce really enhances the beef to make it a dish worthy of company. You'll want to start preparing the sauce toward the end of the braising time and can use the deeply flavorful broth from the braise in place of the chicken or beef stock called for here. Use any leftover sauce on steak or pork chops or spoon it over poached eggs. —AS

3 tablespoons unsalted butter

3 large shallots, thinly sliced

3 garlic cloves, finely chopped

1 pound small wild mushrooms, such as chanterelles, lobster mushrooms, porcinis, or a combination, roughly chopped

¼ cup brandy

¼ cup Worcestershire sauce

1 cup chicken or beef stock

1 teaspoon kosher salt, plus more for seasoning

1 teaspoon freshly ground black pepper, plus more for seasoning

2 tablespoons finely chopped fresh thyme

1. In a medium saucepan set over medium heat, warm 2 tablespoons of the butter until it turns blond. Add the shallots and cook, stirring frequently, until lightly caramelized, about 5 minutes. Add the garlic and cook, stirring frequently, until fragrant and lightly browned, about 1 minute.

2. Add the mushrooms to the pan and stir to incorporate. Cover the pan and cook, stirring occasionally, until the natural juices release from the mushrooms to create a sauce base, 2 to 3 minutes. Add the brandy and cook, stirring occasionally, until the brandy is nearly absorbed, about 1 minute. Add the Worcestershire and cook for 1 minute more to let the flavors blend.

3. Raise the heat to high and add the stock, salt, and pepper to the pan. Cook, stirring occasionally, until the sauce has thickened and reduced by about one-quarter and there is an equal ratio of liquid to mushrooms in the pan, about 5 minutes. Add the remaining 1 tablespoon butter and the thyme to the pan and swirl the pan to incorporate. Remove the sauce from the heat and season with salt and pepper.

Mustard and Hazelnut Crusted Tri-Tip

Serves 6 to 8

Tri-tip isn't usually my favorite cut of the cow, but this simple preparation pleases me every time. Using mustard as a marinade helps the hazelnut-herb crust adhere to the beef and lends the semi-marbled cut a nice bite. —AS

1 cup hazelnuts, toasted and skinned (see Chef's Note)

¼ cup finely chopped fresh sage leaves

¼ cup finely chopped fresh thyme

Kosher salt and freshly ground black pepper

3 pounds tri-tip

⅓ cup Dijon mustard

1. Arrange a rack in the center of the oven and preheat the oven to 425°F. Line a large baking pan with parchment paper.

2. In the bowl of a food processor fitted with the steel blade, pulse the hazelnuts until finely ground but not yet a paste. Transfer the ground nuts to a small bowl. Add the sage, thyme, and a pinch of salt and pepper and stir to combine. Spread the hazelnut-herb mixture over the prepared baking pan. Set aside.

3. Season the tri-tip with salt, then generously coat it on all sides with the mustard. Place the tri-tip in the baking pan and roll it in the hazelnut-herb mixture to coat. Let the tri-tip sit at room temperature for 20 minutes.

4. Transfer the tri-tip to a large broiler pan or a large rimmed baking sheet topped with a cooking rack and cook for 40 minutes or until the tri-tip starts to sweat and the crust is golden brown.

5. Remove the tri-tip from the oven and transfer to a wire rack to rest for 7 minutes. Transfer the tri-tip to a cutting board and thinly slice across the grain. Dig in.

Chef's Note: To toast and skin hazelnuts, arrange a rack in the center of the oven and preheat the oven to 325°F. Spread the hazelnuts on a rimmed baking sheet and bake for 20 to 30 minutes or until they are a rich dark brown and their skins are beginning to fall off. Let the hazelnuts cool slightly and then transfer them to a clean, dry dishtowel and rub the nuts together to remove the remaining skins.

Chard and Goat Cheese Stuffed Lamb Meatballs

Serves 4 to 6

I make these meatballs nearly as big as a baseball and stuff them with fresh goat cheese and sautéed chard. All you really need to serve them is a simple marinara sauce. If you want to round out the meal, serve the meatballs on top of a bed of buttered noodles. —AS

¼ cup finely ground homemade bread crumbs

¼ cup whole milk

1½ pounds ground lamb

1 tablespoon dried basil

1 tablespoon dried oregano

1 tablespoon garlic powder

2 teaspoons kosher salt, plus more for seasoning

2 tablespoons extra-virgin olive oil

1 bunch Swiss chard, stems removed and leaves roughly chopped

Freshly ground black pepper

2 ounces fresh goat cheese

1. Arrange a rack in the center of the oven and preheat the oven to 350°F. Line a large baking sheet with parchment paper.

2. In a small bowl or glass measuring cup, combine the bread crumbs with the milk and set aside to soak for 5 minutes.

3. Transfer the bread crumb mixture to a large bowl and add the lamb, basil, oregano, garlic powder, and salt. Mix using your hands or a rubber spatula until combined. Cover the bowl with plastic wrap and refrigerate until ready to use.

4. In a large skillet set over medium heat, warm the oil. Add the chard and cook, stirring occasionally, until wilted and tender, about 10 minutes. Remove the skillet from the heat. Season with salt and pepper.

5. Divide the meat mixture into six equal-size meatballs. Split each meatball in half and flatten each half to form a patty. Place six of the patties on a clean work surface. Divide the chard and goat cheese evenly among the patties, leaving a ½-inch border around the edges. Cover each of the filled patties with a plain patty. Seal the edges and gently reshape the patties into meatballs.

6. Arrange the meatballs on the prepared baking sheet and bake for 30 minutes or until browned and cooked through. Dig in.

Grilled Lamb Leg Steaks with Balsamic-Braised Figs

Serves 4

Nothing says late, lazy summer day like a grilled lamb leg steak served with the first harvest of figs. I braise the figs in balsamic vinegar and Pinot Noir because they are natural matches for lamb and because the first figs of the season are usually a little firm and need some coaxing to turn juicy. Do yourself a favor and serve this dish on a bed of Creamed Corn (page 221). The creamed corn acts as a binder between the lamb and figs and offers a creamy, sweet finish. —AS

6 juniper berries, crushed

3 tablespoons extra-virgin olive oil

3 teaspoons finely chopped fresh thyme

4 (½-inch-thick) lamb leg steaks (about 2 pounds)

Kosher salt

½ cup balsamic vinegar

½ cup fruity red wine, such as Pinot Noir

6 whole black peppercorns

8 fresh black Mission figs

1. In a large bowl, combine the juniper berries, oil, and 1½ teaspoons of the thyme. Season the lamb steaks with salt. Coat the lamb steaks generously with the juniper berry mixture on both sides, leaving them in the bowl. Cover the bowl with plastic wrap and refrigerate for at least 2 hours or up to overnight.

2. Meanwhile, in a medium saucepan, combine the vinegar, wine, remaining 1½ teaspoons thyme, and the peppercorns and simmer over low heat until reduced by half, about 30 minutes. Strain the balsamic reduction into a bowl to remove the peppercorns and set aside.

3. When the mixture is nearly reduced, arrange a rack in the center of the oven and preheat the oven to 350°F. Place the figs in a small baking pan and pour the balsamic reduction over the figs. Bake the figs for 25 minutes or until they are soft to the touch and the reduction is syrupy. Turn the oven off and let the figs rest in the oven until ready to serve.

4. Meanwhile, when the lamb steaks are ready, line a large baking sheet with parchment paper. Remove the lamb steaks from the refrigerator, transfer to the prepared baking sheet, and let rest until they come up to room temperature, about 45 minutes.

5. Prepare a medium-hot fire in a charcoal grill. Arrange the lamb steaks on the grill rack over direct heat, cover, and grill until they are medium-rare and start to sweat and caramelize on the sides, about 5 minutes per side. Transfer the lamb steaks to a wire rack to rest for 5 minutes.

6. Arrange the lamb steaks on a large serving platter. Spoon the figs and sauce over the top and serve.

Bread Pudding–Stuffed Lamb Shoulder

Serves 8

By the time summer ends, I've had my fill of fresh tomatoes and pole beans. That's when I start wanting the flavors and textures of fall dishes like bread pudding and stuffing. Here, I feed my cool-weather cravings by stuffing an herb-crusted lamb shoulder with a rich bread pudding. This dish is especially great for entertaining during the holidays because it cooks up beautifully and provides you with an elegant centerpiece. If you aren't comfortable butterflying the lamb shoulder yourself, ask your butcher to do it for you. —AS

Lamb Shoulder

1 (4-pound) boneless lamb shoulder, butterflied

3 tablespoons ground fennel seed

2 tablespoons kosher salt

1 tablespoon ground coriander

1 tablespoon finely chopped fresh thyme

½ teaspoon chili flakes

2 large eggs

½ cup heavy cream

1 tablespoon herbes de Provence (without lavender)

1 tablespoon onion powder

2 teaspoons kosher salt

1 teaspoon ground celery seed

1 teaspoon garlic powder

1 teaspoon lemon pepper

1 tablespoon unsalted butter

½ medium yellow onion, finely chopped

2 medium celery stalks, peeled, trimmed, and finely chopped (see Chef's Note, page 93)

1 large carrot, peeled, trimmed, and finely chopped

1 (½-pound) loaf crusty white bread, cut into ½-inch cubes and dried (see Chef's Note)

continued on page 196

1. **Make the lamb shoulder:** Place the lamb shoulder on a cutting board and cover the top with three layers of plastic wrap. Using a meat mallet, pound it until it is 1 inch thick. In a small bowl, combine the fennel seed, salt, coriander, thyme, and chili flakes and whisk to combine. Liberally massage the spice mixture into the lamb shoulder to season all sides. Let the lamb shoulder rest at room temperature for at least 20 minutes or up to 1 hour to let the seasoning penetrate the meat.

2. **Meanwhile, make the bread pudding:** In a large bowl, combine the eggs and cream and whisk to combine. Add the herbes de Provence, onion powder, 1 teaspoon of the salt, the celery seed, garlic powder, and lemon pepper and whisk to combine. Set aside.

3. In a large skillet set over medium heat, warm the butter until it melts. Add the onion, celery, carrot, and remaining 1 teaspoon salt and cook, stirring occasionally, until the carrot and celery soften and the onion is translucent, about 5 minutes. Remove the skillet from the heat and set aside to cool for a few minutes. Add the cooled vegetables and bread cubes to the egg mixture and stir with a wooden spoon to combine. Set aside.

4. When the lamb shoulder is done resting, arrange a rack in the center of the oven and preheat the oven to 350°F. Line a large rimmed baking sheet with parchment paper and place a roasting rack on top. Cut eight 8-inch strands of butcher's twine and set aside. Position the lamb shoulder with the butterflied side up and with the long side facing you. Spread an even layer of the bread pudding, about 1 inch thick, over the lamb shoulder, leaving about a 1-inch border around the edges. Gently roll the lamb shoulder away from you, using even pressure while keeping the pudding mixture inside the roll as snug as possible. Continue rolling the lamb shoulder until you've reached the end.

5. Position the roll seam-side down. Starting at one end of the roll, about 1 inch from the end, slide a piece of twine under the roll and tie the string very tightly around the lamb. Repeat the process with the remaining strands of butcher's twine, spacing the ties equally along the roll.

6. Once the roll is tied, place it on the roasting rack and roast for 1 hour 30 minutes to 2 hours or until the top is nicely browned and slightly crisp. (If you stick a fish fork into the center of the meat and pull it out, the fork should be warm to the touch.)

7. Remove the lamb from the oven and let it rest at room temperature for 10 minutes. Cut off and discard the twine. Using a serrated knife, cut the lamb roll into ½- to 1-inch-thick slices and transfer to a large serving platter. Dig in.

Chef's Note: To dry out the bread cubes, spread the cubes on a baking sheet and let them sit out at room temperature overnight.

Porchetta

Serves 8

I've eaten porchetta at restaurants from coast to coast and still think the version I serve on our Whole Hog plate at The Cat is my favorite way to prepare it. I pay respect to the meat by letting it cure for a full five days; the cure needs that long to season the pork belly throughout and give it the complex flavor and caramelization I'm after. Slices of the porchetta are great with salads or South Carolina Creamy Grits (page 220) for dinner. Use any leftovers in hashes, soups, and sandwiches.

You can preorder a large pork belly through a local butcher or a farmers' market vendor. (You're after a belly from a Duroc pig because they are longer and leaner; pork belly from any other breed will be too fatty for this dish.) Look for curing salt at a specialty store like The Meadow, which has locations in Portland and New York City as well as an online shop. The curing salt I use is called Prague Powder No. 1 and has a slightly pink tint. —AS

2 garlic cloves, finely chopped

2 tablespoons finely chopped fresh flat-leaf parsley

2 tablespoons finely chopped fresh sage leaves

2 tablespoons finely chopped fresh thyme

1 tablespoon ground fennel seed

1 tablespoon ground coriander

1 tablespoon juniper berries, finely ground

1 tablespoon plus 1½ teaspoons kosher salt

1 tablespoon freshly ground black pepper

2 teaspoons ground ginger

2 teaspoons curing salt

1 teaspoon cayenne pepper

1 (5-pound) pork belly

1. In a medium bowl, combine the garlic, parsley, sage, thyme, fennel seed, coriander, juniper berries, kosher salt, pepper, ginger, curing salt, and cayenne and stir to combine. Place the pork belly in a large plastic tub or large nonreactive roasting pan and liberally massage the spice mixture into the meat to season all sides. Cover the pork belly with plastic wrap and refrigerate for 2½ days. Flip the pork belly, cover, and refrigerate for 2½ days more.

2. Arrange a rack in the center of the oven and preheat the oven to 350°F. Remove the pork belly from the tub or pan and place it on a clean work surface, skin-side down and with the long side closest to you. Using a boning knife, make a vertical incision, ¼ inch deep, from the top of the belly to the bottom. Using the vertical incision as a guide, put your fingers under the cut edge and gently cut the meat away with the boning knife, leaving a ¼-inch

border at the far edge of the pork belly so it stays in one long piece. (You are butterflying the pork belly and opening it up like a book.) Repeat the process on the other side. You should now have one long, rectangular piece of pork belly measuring roughly 12 by 24 inches.

3. Cut eight 8-inch strands of butcher's twine and set aside. Working with the pork belly butterflied-side up with the long side closest to you, tightly roll it away from you until you've reached the end and made a long pinwheel.

4. Position the roll seam-side down. Starting at one end of the roll, about 1 inch from the end, slide a piece of twine under the roll and tie the string tightly around the meat. Repeat the process with the remaining strands of butcher's twine, spacing the ties 1 inch apart along the roll.

5. Line a large baking sheet with parchment paper and place a roasting rack on top. Place the porchetta on the roasting rack and roast for 2 hours to 2 hours 30 minutes or until it is dark amber and firm to the touch. (If you stick a fish fork into the center of the meat and pull it out, the fork should be warm to the touch.)

6. Remove the porchetta from the oven and let it rest at room temperature for 30 minutes. Using a large chef's knife, cut the porchetta into 1-inch-thick slices, cutting and removing the twine as you go. Transfer the slices to a large serving platter and dig in.

Brined and Grilled Pork Chops

Serves 4

Most people think pork chops are fatty, but they are actually one of the leanest cuts of the whole animal. Brining tenderizes, plumps, and seasons the meat all the way through. To make sure you get a nicely marbled chop, ask your butcher for a cut that comes from close to the shoulder. Serve these salty-sweet chops with a salad and Mashed Potatoes (page 224), Pecan Spoonbread (page 222) and Smoky Bacon-Braised Collard Greens (page 211) or our Olive Oil–Braised Pole Beans (page 213), and cornbread on the side. —AS

1 cup packed light brown sugar

¾ cup kosher salt

1 tablespoon whole black peppercorns

1 tablespoon chili flakes

1 tablespoon ground coriander

1 tablespoon ground fennel seed

1 tablespoon juniper berries

1 tablespoon finely chopped fresh thyme

4 allspice berries

2 whole cloves

½ cinnamon stick

Finely grated zest and freshly squeezed juice of 1 orange

4 (10-ounce) bone-in pork chops

1. In a medium saucepan, combine 1 quart water, the sugar, salt, peppercorns, chili flakes, coriander, fennel seed, juniper berries, thyme, allspice berries, cloves, cinnamon stick, orange zest, and orange juice. Bring to a boil over medium-high heat.

2. Place 4 cups ice in a nonreactive plastic or metal pan big enough to hold the brine and the pork chops. Stir in the brine. Once the ice melts and the brine comes down to room temperature, place the pork chops in the brine, cover with plastic wrap, and refrigerate for at least 6 hours or up to 24 hours.

3. Line a large baking sheet with parchment paper. Remove the pork chops from the brine and set them on the baking sheet to rest until they dry and come up to room temperature, about 1 hour.

4. When the pork chops are nearly ready, prepare a fire in a charcoal grill and let it burn down to glowing coals. Move the coals to one side of the grill and place the grill grate 6 inches above the coals. Let the grill grate get hot, then place the pork chops on the grill over indirect heat, cover, and grill until firm to the touch and caramelized, 5 to 7 minutes per side. Transfer the lamb steaks to a wire rack to rest for 5 minutes.

5. Transfer the pork chops to a large beautiful serving platter and dig in.

Hickory-Smoked Pork Shoulder

Serves 4 to 6

When you cook a meat in fat, you'll end up with a more luscious and more thoroughly seasoned cut than you'll get from any other cooking method. Here, I cook a hickory-smoked pork shoulder low and slow in duck fat, then break the meat into big hunks to serve with South Carolina Creamy Grits (page 220) and Smoky Bacon-Braised Collard Greens (page 211). —AS

2 tablespoons packed light brown sugar

1 tablespoon kosher salt

1 tablespoon finely chopped fresh sage leaves

1 tablespoon finely chopped fresh thyme

1 teaspoon freshly ground black pepper

1 teaspoon ground fennel seed

1 (3-pound) bone-in pork shoulder

1 cup hickory wood chips, for smoking

2 quarts duck fat

1. In a small bowl, combine the sugar, salt, sage, thyme, pepper, and fennel seed. Place the pork shoulder on a cutting board and liberally massage the spice-herb mixture into all sides. Transfer the pork shoulder to a large plate and let sit at room temperature for 2 hours.

2. Meanwhile, soak the hickory chips according to the package instructions and preheat a smoker to 200°F (or see "Smoking Without a Smoker," page 35). Smoke the pork shoulder for 1 hour. Remove the pork shoulder and set aside.

3. Arrange a rack in the center of the oven and preheat the oven to 350°F. In a large Dutch oven set over low heat, warm the duck fat until it melts. Submerge the smoked pork shoulder, fat-side up, in the melted duck fat and set the Dutch oven on a large rimmed baking sheet. Bake the pork for 3 hours or until fork-tender.

4. Transfer the pork shoulder to a cutting board. Using two forks, pull the pork shoulder apart into big hunks. (Do not shred it.) Transfer the pork shoulder to a large platter and dig in.

THE WHOLE HOG

I go from head to tail on every animal I bring into The Country Cat. The pig was the first beast that helped me share my "use everything, waste nothing" philosophy with the masses because it's approachable in every way. All my favorite parts go into a plate we call The Whole Hog.

When I get a pig on the butcher's block, I think about how it moved through its day when it was alive, and consider the purpose and function of each muscle group. I feel it's my duty as a chef to understand everything that the animal provided to us in order to cook it with integrity and respect and bring out the best flavor and texture in each cut.

I start by brining the head for five days, then simmering it with onions, carrots, and celery to make headcheese croquettes. I remove the luscious meat by hand, chop it up with the vegetables, and mix it with the broth. Then I cool it in a baking dish until it sets, cut it into squares, toss it in a cornmeal mix, and fry it for the plate. Because the shoulder muscle consists of strong muscle fibers that support the neck and head of the animal, I've learned it needs time to break down. So I cook my pork shoulder low and slow until the braised meat is fork-tender. The pliable belly becomes porchetta. I butterfly it, cure it, roll it up, and roast it. Then

I slice it and crisp it in the pan to order. When I'm butchering the loin, I leave it attached to the rib so I can put a showstopper of a tomahawk chop on the plate. I brine those chops before I grill them so they stay nice and juicy and fully seasoned.

When you embrace whole animal cooking like this, it pays off in a number of ways. By making the investment to purchase a whole animal, it will save you money because choice cuts like the coppa and bone-in loin chops are cheaper purchased as part of the whole animal instead of bought individually from a butcher. Buying the whole animal also supports local ranchers and farmers and is better for the environment because the animal didn't have to travel as many miles to get to your plate.

If you plan on making the jump to whole-animal purchasing, think about how you will store it and the space you will need. Many people purchase animals with friends or extended family and then divide the meat among households. Look for local meat collectives in your area where you can purchase whole animals as well as learn how to use and cook each piece. With a whole or even half a hog in your freezer, you can try each one of these recipes separately or together to create your own version of The Whole Hog at home. —AS

In my element breaking down a side of pork.

Brown Butter, Maple Syrup, and Orange Glazed Carrots, page 210

SOMETHIN' FOR THE SIDE

Side dishes offer a chance to complement a main course. They should be a companion to the meal but not steal the thunder. My favorite sides are those you can present in a beautiful bowl or platter and pass around the dinner table so everyone can fill their plate just the way they want. I also like to push the boundaries a little by adding unexpected ingredients to otherwise classic dishes, be it a brown butter glaze for carrots or blackberries in a succotash. To me, sides with an element of surprise enhance the whole dining experience. —AS

Brown Butter, Maple Syrup, and Orange Glazed Carrots

Serves 4

I'm always trying to figure out inventive side dishes that make use of the few vegetables available to me in the winter months. In the past, I've made maple-glazed carrots and orange-glazed carrots to introduce some bright flavors into a winter diet. This dish combines those two recipes and ties their flavors together with brown butter and fresh herbs. —AS

4 tablespoons (½ stick) unsalted butter

¼ cup freshly squeezed orange juice

¼ cup pure maple syrup

1 pound medium carrots, unpeeled, trimmed

2 tablespoons finely chopped fresh sage leaves

2 tablespoons finely chopped fresh thyme

1 teaspoon kosher salt, plus more for seasoning

1. In a large-lidded skillet set over medium heat, melt the butter. Cook, whisking frequently, until the butter solids are brown and start to smell nutty, about 5 minutes.

2. Add the orange juice and maple syrup to the skillet and whisk to combine. Add the carrots and toss to coat. Add ¼ cup water and the sage, thyme, and salt. Bring to a boil. Reduce the heat to low, cover the skillet, and cook until the carrots are tender when pierced with the tip of a knife, about 15 minutes.

3. Remove the skillet from the heat and transfer the carrots to a serving platter, keeping the liquid in the pan. Return the pan to the stove, raise the heat to high, and cook until the liquid is syrupy, about 5 minutes. Spoon the sauce over the carrots. Season with salt and dig in.

Smoky Bacon-Braised Collard Greens

Serves 4

When you're making collard greens, you're dealing with the toughest, most resilient greens out there. You need to be heavy handed with the vinegar, fat, and salt if you want them to break down. We use our housemade Smoky Bacon (page 62) to deliver plenty of fat, and we season the greens heavily with salt, apple cider vinegar, and sherry vinegar. Then we cook them low and slow to produce tender greens and the best by-product of any cooking process: the lip-smacking broth Southerners call "pot likker." If you keep the broth after eating the collard greens, you can serve it like you would any brothy soup. Or just drink it. Seriously—it's that good. —AS

2 tablespoons unsalted butter

6 thick-cut bacon slices, halved lengthwise and roughly chopped

2 medium yellow onions, thinly sliced

2 quarts chicken stock

½ cup apple cider vinegar

½ cup sherry vinegar

Kosher salt and freshly ground black pepper

2 bunches collard greens, stems removed and leaves cut into 1-inch pieces

1. In a large stockpot set over medium heat, warm the butter until it melts. Add the bacon and cook, stirring occasionally, until crispy, about 5 minutes. Transfer the bacon to a small bowl, leaving the fat behind in the pot. Set the bacon aside.

2. Add the onions to the pot and cook, stirring occasionally, until soft and lightly caramelized, about 8 minutes. Return the bacon to the pot, add the stock, apple cider vinegar, and sherry vinegar, and bring the mixture to a simmer. Season with salt and pepper.

3. When the liquid begins to simmer, add the collard greens and stir to combine. Reduce the heat to low, cover, and cook, stirring occasionally, until the collard greens are very tender, about 2 hours 30 minutes.

4. Using a pair of tongs, transfer the collard greens to a medium serving bowl, leaving the liquid behind. Using a slotted spoon, transfer as much bacon as possible to the bowl. (Discard the liquid or reserve for another use.) Dig in.

Olive Oil–Braised Pole Beans

Serves 4

I grew up eating pole beans that were braised with bacon and onions until they nearly fell apart, and that's still my favorite way to prepare them. (To this day, raw pole beans and quickly blanched pole beans just taste wrong to me.) I prefer to cook my pole beans low and slow in olive oil until they are soft and tender. Serve them with any grilled meat or, in true Midwest style, with Skillet-Fried Chicken (page 156). —AS

1 medium yellow onion, thinly sliced

½ medium fennel bulb, thinly sliced

4 garlic cloves, thinly sliced

Peel of 1 lemon

¾ cup extra-virgin olive oil

Kosher salt and freshly ground black pepper

2 fresh thyme sprigs

2 fresh flat-leaf parsley sprigs

1 fresh rosemary sprig

1 dried bay leaf

1 pound pole beans, trimmed

2 cups vegetable stock

Freshly squeezed juice of ½ lemon

1. In a medium stockpot, combine the onion, fennel, garlic, lemon peel, oil, and ¼ cup water. Season with salt and pepper, cover, and simmer over medium heat, stirring occasionally, until the vegetables are translucent, about 15 minutes.

2. Tie the thyme sprigs, parsley sprigs, and rosemary sprig together with butcher's twine to make a bouquet garni. Add the bouquet garni and the bay leaf to the vegetables. Add the pole beans, stock, and lemon juice and stir to combine. Season with salt and pepper. Bring the mixture to a simmer, cover, and cook, stirring occasionally, until the pole beans are very tender, about 1 hour 30 minutes. Remove and discard the bay leaf and bouquet garni. Season with salt and pepper.

3. Using a pair of tongs, transfer the pole beans and vegetables to four plates or to one large serving plate. Dig in.

Asparagus Casserole

Serves 4 to 6

Growing up, my mom made asparagus casserole using a recipe from an old church cookbook. It called for evaporated milk, canned asparagus, and hard-cooked eggs, and I loved it. Years ago, I decided to create my own version, elevating this side dish with fresh asparagus and morels. The result is this lighter, looser casserole topped with crispy bacon and hard-boiled eggs. It's great with our Hickory-Smoked Pork Shoulder (page 203) or "Sappy Spice" Grilled Chicken (page 159). If you can't find morels, you can use big button mushrooms or King oyster mushrooms instead. (Cut the mushrooms into ¼-inch slices and skip step 3 if you use something other than morels.) —AS

4 large eggs

Kosher salt

½ pound fresh morel mushrooms

1 tablespoon unsalted butter

4 thick-cut bacon slices, cut crosswise into ½-inch pieces

3 teaspoons kosher salt, plus more for seasoning

1¼ teaspoons herbes de Provence (without lavender)

¼ teaspoon freshly ground black pepper, plus more for seasoning

¼ teaspoon chili flakes

Finely grated zest of 2 lemons

1 medium yellow onion, finely chopped

4 garlic cloves, thinly sliced

2½ pounds asparagus, trimmed and cut into ½-inch pieces

1 cup heavy cream

3 tablespoons all-purpose flour

1. Place the eggs in a small saucepan and fill with cold water to completely cover the eggs. Salt the water and bring it to a hard simmer over medium-high heat. Once the water reaches a hard simmer, cook the eggs for 8 minutes.

2. Drain the eggs in a colander and run cool water over them. While they are still hot, peel the eggs one by one under cool running water.

3. Meanwhile, bring a medium saucepan of salted water to a boil. Add the morels and boil for 10 seconds. (This cleans the morels and kills any worms or spores that might be in them.) Using a slotted spoon, transfer the morels to a cutting board and pat dry. Halve the morels lengthwise and set aside.

4. Arrange a rack in the center of the oven and preheat the oven to 350°F. Line a small plate with paper towels. In a medium saucepan, melt the butter over medium heat. Add the bacon and cook, stirring occasionally, until crispy, about 5 minutes. Using a slotted spoon, transfer the bacon

continued on page 216

to the paper towel–lined plate and set aside. Remove the saucepan from the heat and remove all but ¼ cup of the rendered bacon fat from the saucepan. (You can discard the remaining bacon fat or reserve it for another use.)

5. Return the saucepan to the stove and set over medium-high heat. Add the morels and 2 teaspoons of the salt and cook, stirring occasionally, until the morels start to release their liquid, about 3 minutes. Add the herbes de Provence, pepper, chili flakes, and lemon zest and stir to combine.

6. Cook, stirring occasionally, until the liquid released from the morels begins to evaporate and the morels are starting to get a little caramelization going, about 3 minutes more. Add the onion and garlic and stir to combine. Cook, stirring occasionally, until softened and golden brown, about 5 minutes more. Add the asparagus and remaining 1 teaspoon salt and stir to combine.

Reduce the heat to medium, cover the saucepan, and cook, stirring occasionally, until the asparagus is slightly tender but not mushy, about 10 minutes more.

7. Add the cream and raise the heat to medium-high. Bring the mixture to a simmer. Using a sifter or fine-mesh strainer, sift the flour over the asparagus mixture in the saucepan. Stir to incorporate and season with additional salt and pepper. Cook, stirring occasionally, until the cream thickens, 1 to 2 minutes. Pour the mixture into an 8-inch square baking pan or casserole dish.

8. Quarter the hard-boiled eggs lengthwise and lay them evenly over the top of the asparagus mixture. Top the casserole with the reserved bacon pieces and season with pepper. Transfer the dish to the oven and bake for 20 minutes to allow the flavors to blend. Remove the casserole from the oven, scoop, and serve.

Chanterelle and Blackberry Succotash

Serves 6

I'm not a purist when it comes to succotash. I put a Pacific Northwest spin on the classic dish by incorporating chanterelle mushrooms and blackberries into the mix, and I add cream because, well, why the hell not? The corn-infused cream gives the dish a great texture and helps carry the flavors through every bite. Served with grilled fish, poultry, or meat, this is my favorite late-summer side dish. —AS

2 large ears corn

1 cup heavy cream

1 tablespoon unsalted butter

3 thick-cut bacon slices, cut crosswise into thin strips

1 medium yellow onion, finely chopped

1 (15-ounce) can pinto beans, drained and rinsed

¼ pound fresh chanterelle mushrooms, large ones halved

Kosher salt and freshly ground black pepper

3 tablespoons roughly chopped fresh flat-leaf parsley

1 lemon, halved

½ pint (about 1 cup) fresh blackberries

1. Using a sharp knife, remove the corn kernels from the cobs and set aside. In a medium bowl, stand a scraped corncob on one end. Using the back side of a chef's knife, scrape the cob to release the residual liquid and corn pulp. Repeat with the remaining corncob, then transfer the liquid and pulp to a small saucepan. (You should have roughly 2 tablespoons pulp and liquid. Discard the corncobs.)

2. Add the cream and cook over medium-low heat, stirring occasionally, until the mixture has thickened slightly and reduced by one-quarter, about 10 minutes. Set aside.

3. Meanwhile, in a large skillet set over medium heat, warm the butter until it melts. Add the bacon and cook, stirring occasionally, until crisp, about 5 minutes. Remove the skillet from the heat and drain half of the rendered fat. (You should have about 1 tablespoon remaining.) Return the skillet to the heat and add the onion. Cook, stirring occasionally, until soft and translucent, about 5 minutes.

4. Add the corn kernels, pinto beans, and chanterelles to the skillet and cook, stirring frequently, until warmed through, about 3 minutes. Season with salt and pepper.

5. Add the reserved warm corn-cream mixture to the skillet and simmer until it has reduced slightly and starts to thicken and really hug the vegetables, about 3 minutes. Stir in the parsley and season with salt, pepper, and lemon juice. Transfer the succotash to a serving platter and garnish with the blackberries. Dig in.

South Carolina Creamy Grits

Serves 4

Grits are really simple to make; the success lies in the technique. A lot of recipes call for bringing the liquid to a boil, then whisking in the grits. I like to combine all the ingredients in a stockpot, then bring the liquid and the grits to a boil together because I've found the grits cook more evenly that way. I also believe that the only grits worth eating are heavily seasoned. And baby, they should be buttery, so don't even think about cutting back on the stick of butter I call for here.

Everyone has their favorite brand of grits. Mine happens to be Charleston Favorites stone-ground grits, but you can use whatever brand you like. —AS

1 cup medium-coarse ground white grits

1 tablespoon kosher salt, plus more for seasoning

8 tablespoons (1 stick) unsalted butter, cut into ½-inch cubes

Freshly ground black pepper

1. In a medium stockpot, combine the grits, 6 cups cold water, and the salt. Whisk the mixture vigorously and let stand for 30 seconds, then use a fine-mesh sieve to skim off any chaff that floats to the surface.

2. Add the butter to the stockpot and bring to a boil over medium-high heat, whisking frequently and vigorously to keep the grits from sticking. Reduce the heat to low and simmer the grits, whisking frequently, until they are very creamy, about 2 hours. (If the grits become too thick before they are creamy, thin them with a bit of hot water as they are cooking.)

3. Season the grits with salt and pepper. Transfer the grits to a medium serving bowl or divide among four plates and dig in.

Creamed Corn

Serves 4

Like many Americans, I grew up eating creamed corn from a can. This scratch-made version always surprises people with its sweet, clean flavor. It makes a good side for chicken, pork, and lamb dishes, especially my Grilled Lamb Leg Steaks with Balsamic–Braised Figs (page 193). But if you ask me, the best way to eat creamed corn is in August and September with late summer tomatoes sliced over the top. —AS

4 large ears corn

2 tablespoons unsalted butter

1 cup heavy cream

2 tablespoons mascarpone cheese

Kosher salt

1. Using a sharp knife, remove the corn kernels from the cobs and set aside. In a medium bowl, stand a scraped corncob on one end. Using the back side of a chef's knife, scrape the cob to release the residual liquid and corn pulp. Repeat with the remaining corncobs and set aside. (You should have roughly ¼ cup pulp and liquid. Discard the corncobs.)

2. In a medium skillet set over medium-high heat, warm the butter until it melts. Add the corn kernels and pulp and cook, stirring occasionally, until they get a little color going, about 3 minutes. Add the cream and cook, stirring occasionally, until the cream has reduced by half, about 6 minutes. Add the mascarpone and stir to incorporate. Remove the skillet from the heat and season with salt. Transfer to a medium bowl and serve.

Pecan Spoonbread

Makes 1 (9 by 13-inch) pan or 12 squares

The next time you go to a potluck, this is a good covered dish to bring. My sweet-savory spoonbread is shot through with bacon and topped with chopped pecans. Because this custardy cornbread tastes best warm with maple syrup poured over the top, I often serve it with our Skillet-Fried Chicken (page 156) at brunch. It also makes a great alternative to regular cornbread.

When it comes time to make the dish, I know it seems counterintuitive to top the wet pudding base with whipped cream before baking it. Don't worry: The spoonbread firms up every time. —AS

1 tablespoon unsalted butter, plus more for greasing the pan

6 thick-cut bacon slices, cut crosswise into thin strips

½ medium yellow onion, finely chopped

2¼ cups (11.25 ounces/321 grams) all-purpose flour

1½ cups (9 ounces/257 grams) finely ground cornmeal

1 tablespoon plus 1½ teaspoons baking powder

1 tablespoon kosher salt

1¼ teaspoons baking soda

½ teaspoon cayenne pepper

5 large eggs

4½ cups whole milk

3 tablespoons granulated sugar

1 tablespoon distilled white vinegar

2¼ cups heavy cream

1 cup roughly chopped pecans

1. Arrange a rack in the center of the oven and preheat the oven to 350°F. Lightly grease a 9 by 13-inch baking pan with butter. Set aside.

2. In a large skillet set over medium heat, warm the butter until it melts. Add the bacon and cook, stirring occasionally, until nearly crisp, about 5 minutes. Add the onion and cook, stirring occasionally, until soft and translucent, about 5 minutes. Set the bacon-onion mixture aside.

3. In a large bowl, combine the flour, cornmeal, baking powder, salt, baking soda, and cayenne and whisk until just combined. In a separate large bowl, combine the eggs, milk, sugar, and vinegar and whisk until combined. Pour the wet mixture into the flour mixture and whisk until just combined. Stir in the reserved bacon-onion mixture and the fat remaining in the skillet (about 2 tablespoons fat). Pour the batter into the prepared baking pan and set aside.

4. In the bowl of a stand mixer fitted with the whisk attachment, beat the cream on medium speed until medium peaks form. Place dollops of the cream over the top of the pudding. Using an offset spatula, gently spread the cream over the top of the pudding to cover. Cover the baking pan tightly with aluminum foil and set it in a larger roasting pan. Pour hot water into the roasting pan to come halfway up the side of the baking pan, creating a hot water bath. Bake the spoonbread for 1 hour.

5. Remove the spoonbread from the oven, uncover, and discard the aluminum foil. Sprinkle the pecans evenly over the top and return the spoonbread to the oven for 30 minutes more or until the center is just set but not dry. Remove the spoonbread from the oven and remove it from the water bath. Let stand for 30 minutes before slicing into squares and digging in.

Mashed Potatoes with Sausage Gravy

Serves 6

At The Cat, we serve mashed potatoes and gravy 365 days a year and tell our cooks to think of the potatoes as the binder for all the sour cream and butter we whip into them. I use sour cream instead of milk in my mashed potatoes because I love the tang it brings to the dish. Leaving the peel on the potatoes gives the dish a bit of color and a rustic look. —AS

2 pounds medium red potatoes, scrubbed and halved

Kosher salt

8 ounces full-fat sour cream

6 tablespoons (¾ stick) unsalted butter, cut into ½-inch cubes

Freshly ground black pepper

Sausage Gravy (opposite), for serving

1. Place the potatoes in a medium stockpot and add cold water to cover. Bring to a high simmer over medium-high heat. Season the water with salt. Simmer until the potatoes are fork-tender, about 15 minutes.

2. Drain the potatoes and transfer them to the bowl of a stand mixer fitted with the whisk attachment. Add the sour cream and butter and whip on low speed for 10 seconds. Raise the speed to high and whip for 10 seconds more. Season with salt and pepper.

3. Divide the mashed potatoes among six plates and, using the back of a large spoon, make a well in each mound of potatoes. Generously ladle gravy over the potatoes and dig in. (Alternatively, you can serve the potatoes family-style in a large bowl and pass the gravy on the side.)

Sausage Gravy

Makes about 2½ cups

When it comes to slow-cooked sauces like this meaty gravy, I always reach for dried herbs because they maintain the integrity of their flavor throughout the cooking process far better than fresh herbs would. I especially like to use herbes de Provence in this gravy because it contributes a lot of the background spices I'm looking for in one ingredient. Just make sure your herbes de Provence doesn't include lavender—you don't want your gravy to taste like your grandmother's neck! —AS

4 thick-cut bacon slices, halved lengthwise and roughly chopped

⅓ pound bulk pork breakfast sausage

1 medium yellow onion, roughly chopped

1 quart chicken stock

1½ tablespoons herbes de Provence (without lavender)

1½ teaspoons chili flakes

1½ teaspoons kosher salt, plus more for seasoning

1 teaspoon freshly ground black pepper, plus more for seasoning

4 tablespoons (½ stick) unsalted butter, cut into ½-inch cubes

6 tablespoons all-purpose flour

1. In a medium saucepan, cook the bacon over medium heat, stirring occasionally, until crisp, about 5 minutes. Add the sausage and cook, stirring occasionally, until browned, about 5 minutes. Add the onion and cook, stirring occasionally, until translucent, about 8 minutes. Add the stock, herbes de Provence, chili flakes, salt, and pepper and bring the mixture to a simmer.

2. Meanwhile, in a medium stockpot set over medium heat, warm the butter until it melts. Add the flour and whisk to combine. Cook, whisking frequently, until the roux is the color of peanut butter, about 10 minutes.

3. Gradually ladle the bacon-sausage mixture into the pot and stir to combine with the roux. Bring the mixture to a simmer over medium heat, stirring occasionally. Simmer, stirring occasionally, until the mixture has thickened enough to coat the back of a spoon, about 20 minutes. Remove the gravy from the heat and season with salt and pepper.

Barley-Quinoa Cakes

Makes 10 (1½-inch) cakes

Most grain-based cakes rely on an egg or two to bind the patties together. Here I take a different approach by using some barley and quinoa as a binder. Be sure to process the grains in the food processor when they are very hot for best results.

These versatile little cakes are great accompaniments to meat dishes, though they are hearty enough to stand on their own as an entrée as well. We also like to serve them with our Smoked Tomato Jam (page 283) and an arugula salad for a light meal. —AS

1 tablespoon unsalted butter

1 small carrot, peeled, trimmed, and finely chopped

1 small celery stalk, peeled, trimmed, and finely chopped (see Chef's Note, page 93)

1 small shallot, finely chopped

1 cup hulled barley

¼ cup dry white wine, such as Chardonnay

3 cups vegetable stock

1 cup multicolor quinoa, rinsed

1 tablespoon apple cider vinegar

1 tablespoon sherry vinegar

¼ cup finely grated Parmesan cheese

1 tablespoon herbes de Provence (without lavender)

2 teaspoons kosher salt, plus more for seasoning

2 tablespoons extra-virgin olive oil

1. In a large stockpot, melt the butter over medium-high heat and cook until blond. Add the carrot, celery, and shallot and cook, stirring occasionally, until translucent, about 5 minutes. Add the barley and toast, stirring occasionally, for 1 minute. Add the wine, then the stock and bring to a boil. Reduce the heat to medium-low and cook the barley, stirring occasionally, until it has absorbed all the liquid and is tender but still has some bite to it, about 45 minutes.

2. Meanwhile, in a large stockpot, combine the quinoa with 2 cups water. Bring the mixture to a boil over medium heat. Reduce the heat to low, cover, and cook until the quinoa pearls and has absorbed all the water, about 15 minutes. Remove the stockpot from the heat and set aside, covered, to keep warm.

3. Transfer half of the barley and vegetables to the bowl of a food processor fitted with the steel blade and puree, scraping the sides of the bowl with a rubber spatula as needed. (The puree will be fairly coarse.) Transfer the puree to the bowl of a stand mixer, add the unpureed barley-vegetable mixture, and set aside.

4. Transfer half of the reserved quinoa to the bowl of the food processor and puree, scraping the sides of the bowl with a rubber spatula as needed. (The puree will have a gummy texture.) Transfer the puree and the remaining quinoa to the bowl of the stand mixer. Add the apple cider vinegar, sherry vinegar, cheese, herbes de Provence, and salt. Using the paddle attachment, mix on medium speed until combined, about 3 minutes. Season with salt.

5. Arrange a rack in the center of the oven and preheat the oven to 350°F. Line a large baking sheet with parchment paper. Using an ice cream scoop, scoop the quinoa-barley mixture out of the bowl and form the scoops into cakes. Place the formed cakes on the prepared baking sheet. (You should have 10 cakes.)

6. In a 12-inch cast-iron skillet set over medium heat, heat the oil until it shimmers. Add the cakes to the skillet and cook until crispy on one side, about 3 minutes. Transfer the skillet to the oven and bake the cakes for 5 minutes. Remove the skillet from the oven, flip the cakes over, and call it a day.

Chef's Note: If you prefer to bake the cakes only, without shallow frying them first, arrange a rack in the center of the oven and preheat the oven to 375°F. Line a large baking sheet with parchment paper and spray the parchment paper with nonstick cooking spray. Shape the grain mixture into 10 patties and arrange them on the baking sheet. Bake the cakes for 15 minutes or until the bottoms are brown. Using a spatula, flip the cakes and bake for about 5 minutes more or until the bottoms are brown on the second side. Remove the baking sheet from the oven and call it a day.

Granny Cris's Stuffing

Makes 1 (9-inch square) baking pan, or 6 to 8 squares

My granny Cris made down-home turkey giblet stuffing by making a flavorful stock with the turkey neck and giblets, then incorporating the tender meat into the stuffing. I loved it, even though it was a little dry and she used cheap white bread to make it. For our first Thanksgiving service at the restaurant, I sought ways to improve her recipe while still maintaining my memory of the original. I quickly found that I prefer soft potato bread to basic white bread. I also add far more eggs to the stuffing than my granny did and use cream in place of the more traditional milk to give my version a custardlike appeal. —AS

1 turkey neck, cut into 8 pieces

¼ pound turkey giblets

1 quart chicken stock

2 tablespoons unsalted butter, at room temperature

4 thick-cut bacon slices, roughly chopped

3 medium carrots, peeled and finely chopped

3 medium celery stalks, peeled, trimmed, and finely chopped (see Chef's Note, page 93)

1 large yellow onion, finely chopped

2 tablespoons dried rubbed sage

2 tablespoons dried thyme

Nonstick cooking spray

8 large eggs

1 cup heavy cream

1 tablespoon kosher salt

2 teaspoons freshly ground black pepper

1 (½-pound) loaf potato bread or white sandwich bread, cut into ½-inch cubes and dried (see Chef's Note, page 196) (about 5 cups)

1. In a medium stockpot, combine the turkey neck, turkey giblets, and stock. Bring the stock to a simmer over medium heat and skim off any impurities that rise to the top with a fine-mesh sieve. Reduce the heat to low and simmer until the turkey meat easily pulls away from the neck with a fork and the giblets are tender, about 2 hours 30 minutes.

2. Strain the stock into a medium bowl and set aside. Transfer the turkey neck and giblets to a cutting board and pull the neck meat off the bone. Roughly chop the neck meat and giblets and let cool to room temperature. Transfer the meat to a small bowl, cover, and refrigerate until ready to use.

3. In a medium stockpot set over medium heat, warm the butter until it melts. Add the bacon and cook, stirring occasionally, until crisp, about 5 minutes. Add the carrots, celery, and onion to the pot and cook, stirring occasionally, until lightly caramelized, about 5 minutes. Add the sage and thyme and stir to combine. Add the

turkey stock and cook until the liquid has reduced by about half, about 15 minutes. Remove the stockpot from the heat and set aside to cool to room temperature.

4. Arrange a rack in the center of the oven and preheat the oven to 350°F. Spray the bottom and sides of a 9-inch square baking pan with nonstick cooking spray and set aside.

5. In a large bowl, combine the eggs, cream, salt, and pepper and whisk until combined. Add the turkey meat and vegetable mixture to the bowl and whisk until combined. Scatter the bread cubes into the dish and pour the turkey-vegetable mixture over the top. Using your hands, massage the mixture into the bread until the bread is well soaked and the mixture is evenly distributed.

6. Transfer the stuffing to the oven and bake for 20 minutes. Rotate the pan and bake for 30 minutes more or until the top of the stuffing is crispy and golden and the custard has been absorbed and set but not dried out. Dig in.

Honey Paprika Potatoes

Serves 4

Years ago, when Jackie and I were falling in love, we found ourselves working at two fine dining restaurants located smack-dab across the street from each other in Northwest Portland. We often shared ideas and inspirations with each other and at some point Jackie mentioned she'd used smoky paprika and honey in a glaze for duck. I liked the idea, so I stole it to dress up crispy home fries like these.

If you can't find ricotta salata, you can serve these potatoes with a generous scoop of fresh ricotta cheese on the side. —AS

3 large red potatoes, cut into ½-inch pieces

3 tablespoons extra-virgin olive oil

2 tablespoons finely chopped fresh rosemary

Kosher salt and freshly ground black pepper

2½ tablespoons honey

2 teaspoons dried oregano

2 teaspoons garlic powder

2 teaspoons smoked paprika

¼ cup ricotta salata cheese

¼ cup fresh flat-leaf parsley, finely chopped

1. Arrange a rack in the center of the oven and preheat the oven to 400°F.

2. In a medium bowl, toss the potatoes with the oil, rosemary, and a pinch of salt and pepper. Transfer the potatoes to a large baking sheet and roast for 30 minutes or until crispy and fork-tender.

3. In a large skillet set over medium heat, warm the honey until it liquefies. Stir in the oregano, garlic powder, and paprika. Add the potatoes to the skillet and toss them in the honey and spices until well coated.

4. Remove the skillet from the heat and transfer the potatoes to a serving dish. Garnish the potatoes with the ricotta salata and parsley and dig in.

Chef's Note: If plain and crispy home fries are more your style, follow the recipe through step 2, then toss the potatoes with 1 teaspoon herbes de Provence (without lavender) and season with salt before digging in.

THE COVERED DISH

When you go to a potluck, church picnic, or bazaar in the Midwest, you bring a covered dish. When guests arrive, they place their dish on a big long table, which is filled with an assortment of Pyrex pieces and hand-me-down servingware. They're all topped with aluminum foil or those plastic lids that are impossible to get off.

Though the covered dish is at the center of any get-together in the Heartland, truth be told, I've never been a fan of potlucks. What you inevitably end up with is a bunch of random dishes that riff on the same thing. (In the Midwest, that would be casserole. You can always count on there being a macaroni casserole, a cornbread casserole, a green bean casserole, baked cheese grits, a ham salad, and dish upon dish topped with potato chips.)

I've learned to endure potlucks by putting some thought into improving the good old covered dish. Growing up, cream-based vegetable

casseroles with a crispy topping were my favorites, so I often favor that combination. When selecting the vegetables, I choose ones that are in season and that taste good when they are slow baked. Green beans, corn, and asparagus are all perfect options for casseroles because they maintain their integrity.

I always add cream and a grated cheese, soft cheese, or a combination of the two to the base because it helps bind the casserole together and also enriches the flavors of the vegetables I'm using. I also like to throw in a bit of bacon to add texture and a smoky flavor. The finishing touch has got to be a crispy topping like onion rings, potato chips, or toasted almonds to counter the soft casserole underneath. Then you've got yourself a winner that will stand out from the other covered dishes in the spread. —AS

A SWEET FINISH

I spent years as a savory cook before transitioning into the pastry kitchen, and because of my training, I don't make cloyingly sweet desserts. Instead, I use good-quality chocolate or fresh, ripe fruit and let the qualities of those ingredients shine through so that you can taste more than just the sugar. I also like to test the boundaries of traditional recipes by throwing in something unexpected—maybe an herb or a bit of booze. Finishing a meal with a surprising little sweet can enhance any family gathering, from a brunch to a BBQ to a dinner. The right dessert can lighten the palate after a hearty meal or offer sinful decadence when it's really time to celebrate. —JS

Bourbon Peach Crumble Pie

Makes 1 (10-inch) pie

There comes a point every summer when peaches are at their peak and I have to stop everything and make peach pie. I like to make crumble pies when I'm working with juicy fruits because the streusel soaks up some of the fruit's juices and gives you the best elements of a crisp and a pie in each slice. I also give those juices a boost in this recipe with a few shots of bourbon because, well, what pairs better with peaches than bourbon? Be sure to serve each slice with a scoop of ice cream on top.

If you must have peach pie when peaches aren't in season, you can make this recipe using 3½ pounds thinly sliced frozen peaches. Be sure to defrost and drain the peaches before using them. —JS

1 (10-inch) pie crust (page 239)

All-purpose flour, for dusting

Crumb Topping

1¼ cups (6.25 ounces/180 grams) all-purpose flour

½ cup (3.75 ounces/107 grams) packed light brown sugar

¼ cup (1.75 ounces/50 grams) granulated sugar

1 tablespoon ground cinnamon

¼ teaspoon kosher salt

8 tablespoons (1 stick) unsalted butter, melted

Peach Filling

4 pounds peaches, halved, pitted, and cut into ½-inch slices (about 8 cups)

1 cup (7 ounces/200 grams) granulated sugar

½ cup (2 ounces/60 grams) cornstarch

3 tablespoons bourbon

2 tablespoons freshly squeezed lemon juice

1. Remove the pie dough from the refrigerator and let it rest, still wrapped, at room temperature for 20 minutes.

2. On a clean, lightly floured work surface, unwrap and roll out the dough into a circle measuring roughly 14 inches in diameter. Gently transfer the rolled dough to a 10-inch deep-dish pie pan, making sure it covers the entire pan and has roughly 1 to 2 inches of dough hanging over the edges. Trim the edges so that 1 inch of dough remains and tuck it underneath the pan edge. Crimp the edges. Poke the base and the sides of the pie shell with a fork and freeze for at least 1 hour or overnight.

3. **Make the crumb topping:** In a large bowl, whisk together the flour, brown sugar, granulated sugar, cinnamon, and salt until combined. Pour the melted butter over the flour mixture and, using your hands, mix until the topping starts to clump and forms big crumbles when you squeeze it. Spread the crumb mixture out on a large baking sheet and let it dry out at room temperature for 30 minutes.

4. Arrange a rack in the center of the oven and preheat the oven to 375°F. Line a large baking sheet with parchment paper and set aside.

5. **Make the peach filling:** In a large bowl, combine the peaches, granulated sugar, cornstarch, bourbon, and lemon juice and mix until combined. Set aside for 10 minutes so the juices can release. Meanwhile, remove the frozen pie shell from the freezer and let it warm up for 10 minutes.

6. Using your hands, scoop the peaches out of the bowl and transfer them to the pie shell. Spoon 2 to 3 tablespoons of the juice remaining in the bowl over the peaches. (Use 2 tablespoons for really juicy peaches and 3 tablespoons for less juicy peaches. Discard any remaining juice.) Top the peaches evenly with the crumb topping.

7. Transfer the pie to the prepared baking sheet and bake for 25 minutes. Reduce the oven temperature to 350°F and bake for 45 minutes to 1 hour more or until the crust is golden brown and the juices are thick and bubbling around the edges. Remove the pie from the oven and let cool on a wire rack for at least 1 hour before slicing and digging in. Stored at room temperature, the pie will keep for up to 2 days.

My Ultimate Pie Crust

Makes 3 (10-inch) pie shells

When I make pie dough, I use my hands—not the sharp blades of a food processor—to gently work the butter into the dough. The key to success is having all your ingredients well chilled and using a light touch so you don't warm the butter too much while you are working the dough. Keep these things in mind and your pie will have a tender, buttery, and perfectly flaky crust every time.

This recipe will make enough dough for three 10-inch pie shells or for the top and bottom of 1 pie plus 1 extra shell. Store any extra pie dough tightly wrapped in plastic wrap in the freezer and use it within 1 month. When you are ready to use it, defrost it overnight in the refrigerator and then let it rest on the counter until it is warm enough to easily roll out but still cooler than room temperature. —JS

5 cups (1 pound 9 ounces/720 grams) all-purpose flour, plus more for dusting

1 tablespoon kosher salt

2 cups (4 sticks) unsalted butter, chilled and cut into ½-inch cubes

1 large egg

1 tablespoon apple cider vinegar

Ice water

1. In a large bowl, combine the flour with the salt. Add the butter and mix it in with your hands until the butter is the size of large peas and the flour has a meal-like consistency. Set aside.

2. In a glass measuring cup, whisk the egg with the vinegar until just combined. Add enough ice water to the egg-vinegar mixture to reach the 1 cup mark. Whisk to combine, then use a fork to gently stir the egg-vinegar mixture into the flour-butter mixture. Using your hands, gently work the dough in the bowl until it starts to come together.

3. Turn out the dough onto a clean, lightly floured work surface and form the dough into a rough rectangle. Take the top third of the dough and fold it down onto itself, then fold the bottom third up onto itself, like you are folding a letter. Pat the dough to bring it together. Give the dough a quarter turn and repeat the folding process. Repeat for a total of five turns. The dough will be a bit ragged but should be combined.

4. Divide the dough into three equal pieces and wrap each piece in plastic wrap. Let the dough rest in the refrigerator for at least 20 minutes or up to 24 hours before using.

Free-Form Apple Pie

Makes 1 (10-inch) pie

This rustic version of an American classic is quicker and easier to make than a traditional pie. It's also a great dish to take to a brunch or dinner party—you won't need to fuss with a pie pan, and you'll find it's far less cumbersome to serve but equally attractive. Serve slices warm with a dollop of thick yogurt on top for brunch, or a scoop of vanilla ice cream and drizzle of caramel sauce for dessert. —JS

1 (10-inch) pie crust (page 239)

All-purpose flour, for dusting

6 medium Granny Smith or Gravenstein apples, peeled, cored, cut into ¼-inch-thick slices, and halved (about 6 cups)

¾ cup (5.25 ounces/150 grams) granulated sugar

3 tablespoons cornstarch

2 tablespoons freshly squeezed lemon juice

1½ tablespoons ground cinnamon

1 large egg

2 tablespoons turbinado sugar

1. Line a large baking sheet with parchment paper. Remove the pie dough from the refrigerator and let it rest, still wrapped, at room temperature for 20 minutes.

2. On a clean, lightly floured work surface, roll the dough into a large, ⅛-inch-thick circle about 14 inches in diameter. Transfer the dough to the prepared baking sheet and set aside.

3. In a large bowl, combine the apples, granulated sugar, cornstarch, lemon juice, and cinnamon and use your hands to mix until the apples are well coated with the mixture. Set aside for 10 minutes at room temperature to let the flavors meld.

4. Using your hands, transfer the apples to the middle of the pie dough, leaving the majority of the juices behind to prevent the bottom of the pie from getting soggy. Spread the apples out in an even circle on the surface of the dough, leaving a 2-inch border around the edge.

5. Viewing the pie like you would a clock, start at the 12 o'clock mark and gently fold a portion of the dough snugly over the apples and over itself to make a nice pleat in the dough. Repeat the folding-and-pleating process, moving clockwise along the edge of the dough, until all the edges of the dough are pleated and folded. (Your pie should be a rustic circle with the apples showing in the center. It will resemble a pizza, just with more crust.)

continued on page 242

6. Transfer the baking sheet to the refrigerator and let the pie rest for 20 minutes. Meanwhile, arrange a rack in the center of the oven and preheat to 375°F.

7. Remove the pie from the refrigerator. In a small bowl or glass measuring cup, combine the egg with 1 tablespoon water and whisk to combine. Using a pastry brush, brush the egg wash over the edges of the pastry. Liberally sprinkle the edges of the pie with the turbinado sugar.

8. Transfer the pie to the oven and bake for 20 minutes. Reduce the oven temperature to 350°F and bake for 30 minutes more or until the crust is golden brown, the juices are thick, and the apples are soft. Remove the pie from the oven and let cool for 20 minutes before slicing and digging in.

Rhubarb Cobbler with Ruby Caramel

Makes 6 (6-ounce) ramekins and about 1 cup caramel

When rhubarb comes back into season each spring, its ruby red stalks are always a welcome sight. When picking rhubarb stalks, the thin, firm, and deep red stalks are best because they are younger and aren't as woody or watery as the big, thick ones. When cooked, they release a beautiful red juice that matches the deep red hue of the ruby caramel in this recipe. I like topping my cobblers with sugar cookie dough as opposed to a traditional biscuit. It's not as heavy and the cookie is easy to cut through when eating. —JS

Sugar Cookie Topping

1⅓ cups (6.7 ounces/192 grams) all-purpose flour

1 teaspoon baking soda

1 teaspoon cream of tartar

½ teaspoon kosher salt

8 tablespoons (1 stick) unsalted butter, softened

¾ cup (5.25 ounces/150 grams) granulated sugar, plus more for dredging

1 large egg

Rhubarb Filling

2 pounds fresh rhubarb, cut into ½-inch pieces

¾ cup (5.25 ounces/150 grams) granulated sugar

¼ cup (2 ounces/57 grams) packed light brown sugar

2 tablespoons cornstarch

1½ teaspoons ground cinnamon

Finely grated zest and freshly squeezed juice of 1 orange

Ruby Caramel

¾ cup (5.25 ounces/150 grams) granulated sugar

½ cup fruity red wine, such as Zinfandel

½ cup heavy cream

Vanilla ice cream, for serving

1. **Make the sugar cookie topping:** In a small bowl, combine the flour, baking soda, cream of tartar, and salt and whisk to combine. Set aside.

2. In the bowl of a stand mixer fitted with the paddle attachment, cream the butter and granulated sugar on high speed until nice and fluffy, 2 to 3 minutes. Scrape down the sides of the bowl with a rubber spatula, then add the egg and mix on medium speed until combined. Add the flour mixture and mix on low speed to combine. Turn out the dough onto a sheet of plastic wrap, shape it into a ball, and wrap tightly. Let the dough rest in the refrigerator for at least 20 minutes or up to overnight.

3. **Meanwhile, make the rhubarb filling:** In a large bowl, combine the rhubarb, granulated sugar, brown sugar, cornstarch, cinnamon, orange zest, and orange juice and use your hands to mix thoroughly to coat the rhubarb. Set aside.

4. Arrange a rack in the center of the oven and preheat the oven to 350°F. Line a large rimmed baking sheet with parchment paper and arrange six 6-ounce ramekins on top. Divide the rhubarb evenly among the ramekins. (The rhubarb will rise over the top of each ramekin but will cook down.)

5. Portion the dough into ten balls. (They should be about the size of a golf ball.) Flatten six of the dough balls into discs and dredge them in granulated sugar. Place one disc on top of the rhubarb in each ramekin. (You can bake the remaining dough balls at 325°F for 10 to 12 minutes to make cookies for another day, or wrap the dough balls in plastic wrap and freeze them for up to 1 month.)

6. Transfer the baking sheet to the oven and bake for 35 to 40 minutes, rotating halfway through, or until the cookie topping is golden and firm to the touch and the juices from the rhubarb are thick and bubbling around the edges. Remove the baking sheet from the oven and let the cobblers cool for 15 minutes.

7. **While the cobblers are cooling, make the ruby caramel:** In a small saucepan, combine the granulated sugar, wine, and 1 tablespoon water. Clip a candy thermometer to the saucepan and bring the mixture to a hard simmer over medium heat. Cook, stirring occasionally, until the wine has reduced by about one-third and the temperature reaches 165°F.

8. Remove the saucepan from the heat and carefully pour in the cream. Gently whisk to combine. Return the saucepan to the stove and cook the caramel over low heat to melt the sugar into the cream and let the cream reduce slightly, 8 to 10 minutes. (Don't let the cream bubble over too much, as it can break.) Remove the saucepan from the heat and set aside. (The caramel will thicken more as it sits.)

9. Place the ramekins on individual dessert plates. Serve the cobbler with scoops of vanilla ice cream and a drizzle of the caramel on the top. (Cool any extra caramel and store it in an airtight container in the refrigerator for up to 2 weeks.)

Rhubarb Cobbler with Ruby Caramel, page 242

Basil-Infused Strawberry Shortcakes, page 248

Basil-Infused Strawberry Shortcakes

Serves 8

My summer is never complete until I dive into a plate of strawberry shortcake while I sit in my backyard enjoying the breeze. I've given this backyard BBQ favorite a playful touch by adding basil to the strawberry topping. That hint of basil gives the dessert an added dimension that tastes of summer to me. —JS

3 cups (15 ounces/432 grams) all-purpose flour, plus more for dusting

¼ cup (2 ounces/57 grams) packed light brown sugar

1½ tablespoons baking powder

¾ teaspoon kosher salt

1 cup (2 sticks) unsalted butter, chilled and cut into ½-inch cubes

2 large eggs

2 tablespoons low-fat buttermilk

¾ teaspoon pure vanilla extract or vanilla bean paste

4 pints fresh strawberries (about 8 cups), hulled and quartered

½ cup (3.5 ounces/100 grams) granulated sugar

1 tablespoon plus 1 teaspoon freshly squeezed lemon juice

8 fresh basil leaves, torn into small pieces

1 tablespoon heavy cream

1 tablespoon turbinado sugar

Whipped cream, for serving

1. In the bowl of a stand mixer fitted with the paddle attachment, combine the flour, brown sugar, baking powder, and salt and mix on medium speed to combine. Add the butter and mix until it is reduced to the size of peas, about 3 minutes. Add the eggs, buttermilk, and vanilla and mix until combined, about 2 minutes.

2. Turn out the dough onto a clean, lightly floured work surface. Press the dough together to form it into a rectangle. Take the far end of the rectangle and fold the dough in half over itself. Press down on the folded mass and give the dough a quarter turn. Repeat the folding-and-turning process for three turns. (This process makes layers in the dough that create nice flaky shortcakes.) Shape the dough into a disc and wrap it in plastic wrap. Let the dough rest in the refrigerator for at least 20 minutes or up to 1 hour.

3. Meanwhile, in a medium bowl, combine the strawberries, granulated sugar, lemon juice, and basil and stir to combine. Cover the bowl with plastic wrap and let the strawberries macerate at room temperature for at least 30 minutes or up to 1 hour.

4. Arrange a rack in the center of the oven and preheat the oven to 350°F. Line a large baking sheet with parchment paper and set aside. Remove the dough from the refrigerator. On a clean, lightly floured work surface, roll out the dough into a ½-inch-thick circle. Cut the circle into eight wedges. Arrange the wedges on the prepared baking sheet. Brush the wedges with the cream and sprinkle with the turbinado sugar. Bake for about 20 minutes or until golden brown on top. Remove the shortcakes from the oven and let cool on the baking sheet for 10 minutes.

5. Cut the shortcakes in half along the equator and place one bottom half on each of eight plates. Spoon the strawberries over the shortcakes, dividing them equally and reserving a few spoonfuls for the top. Top each serving with a generous spoonful of whipped cream. Set the top halves of the shortcakes over the whipped cream and strawberries. Garnish with another dollop of whipped cream and a few more strawberries and serve immediately.

Pear-Gingerbread Upside-Down Cake

Makes 1 (9 by 13-inch) cake

I've got a real thing for upside-down cakes, and I make a lot of seasonal variations—cranberry, rhubarb, lemon, you name it. This dark, molasses-y pear-gingerbread cake is my favorite by far. The pears hold up really well and play perfectly with the warming spices in the cake. Though a lot of gingerbread cakes get better with age, this is one you'll want to eat warm, when it's nice and gooey. Serve thick squares of the cake with a scoop of ice cream as a fancy dinner party dessert, or offer it as an indulgent brunch dish with a pot of coffee on the side. —JS

Caramel and Pears

4 tablespoons (½ stick) unsalted butter, melted

½ cup (3.75 ounces/107 grams) packed light brown sugar

Nonstick cooking spray

3 large firm-ripe Bartlett or Bosc pears, peeled, cored, and cut into ¼-inch-thick slices

Gingerbread Cake

1 cup (11 ounces/314 grams) unsulphured blackstrap molasses

1 teaspoon baking soda

Hot water

2½ cups (12.5 ounces/360 grams) all-purpose flour

1 tablespoon baking powder

2 teaspoons ground cinnamon

2 teaspoons ground ginger

½ teaspoon kosher salt

8 tablespoons (1 stick) unsalted butter, at room temperature

1 cup (7.5 ounces/214 grams) packed light brown sugar

1 large egg

Vanilla ice cream, for serving (optional)

1. **Make the caramel and pears:** Arrange a rack in the center of the oven and preheat the oven to 350°F. Place a 9 by 13-inch baking pan in the oven to warm for 5 minutes.

2. While the pan warms, in a small saucepan , combine the butter with the sugar and heat over medium heat, stirring, until the butter has melted, the sugar has completely dissolved, and a smooth, emulsified caramel forms, 8 to 10 minutes. Remove the baking pan from the oven, spray it with nonstick cooking spray, and pour the caramel into it, spreading it with a rubber spatula to cover the bottom of the pan evenly. Arrange the pears in three overlapping rows on top of the caramel. Set the baking pan aside.

3. **Make the gingerbread cake:** In a medium bowl, combine the molasses, baking soda, and 1½ cups hot water and whisk to combine. Set aside to cool until lukewarm. In a separate medium bowl, combine the flour, baking powder, cinnamon, ginger, and salt and whisk to combine. Set aside.

4. In the bowl of a stand mixer fitted with the paddle attachment or in a bowl using a hand mixer, combine the butter, sugar, and cream on medium speed until fluffy. Add the egg and mix, scraping down the sides of the bowl with a rubber spatula as needed. With the mixer running on medium-low speed, add the cooled molasses mixture in three additions, alternating with the flour mixture. Pour the batter over the pears and spread it evenly with a rubber spatula. Bake the cake for 30 minutes or until a tester stick inserted into the center of the cake comes out clean.

5. Let the cake rest in the pan for 3 minutes. Run a knife around the edge of the cake, then invert it onto a large rectangular serving plate. Leave the pan on top of the cake for 5 minutes to let the pears settle before gently removing it. (If some of the pears stick to the pan, simply rearrange them on the cake.) Cut the cake into squares and serve warm or at room temperature, with ice cream, if desired.

Molly's Toffee

Makes about 1 pound

My sister-in-law and toffee master, Molly Sappington, makes this pecan-topped toffee every holiday season, and we always look forward to getting a tin of it as a gift. It's great to use on cookie plates and as a sundae garnish. —JS

1 cup (2 sticks) unsalted butter, cut into ½-inch cubes

1 cup (7 ounces/200 grams) sugar

½ teaspoon kosher salt

1 cup (8 ounces/228 grams) bittersweet or semisweet chocolate chips

¾ cup (6 ounces/171 grams) roughly chopped pecans, toasted (see Chef's Note, page 55)

1. Line a large baking sheet with parchment paper or a Silpat mat.

2. In a medium saucepan, combine the butter with the sugar and 3 tablespoons water. Cook over medium heat, stirring continuously with a wooden spoon, until the caramel turns a light amber and reaches 300°F on a candy thermometer, about 15 minutes. Immediately pour the caramel onto the prepared baking sheet, tilting the sheet as needed to spread the caramel evenly.

3. Sprinkle the salt evenly over the hot caramel, then sprinkle with the chocolate chips. Let the chocolate chips rest until they start to melt. Using a rubber spatula, gently spread the chocolate chips evenly over the caramel. (Do not stir the chocolate chips into the caramel.) Sprinkle the pecans evenly over the chocolate. Let the toffee sit at room temperature until completely cool and set, about 4 hours.

4. Using your hands, break the toffee into pieces and transfer to an airtight container. Stored at room temperature, the toffee will keep for up to 1 week.

Butterscotch Pudding

Makes 8 (6-ounce) puddings

If Adam's childhood was all about fried chicken, mine was about pudding. The taste of butterscotch pudding especially brings back childhood memories, though I never liked the rubbery character of cornstarch-thickened recipes. Instead, I prefer to thicken my pudding with fresh, high-quality eggs and bake it in a hot water bath to achieve a silky-smooth texture. Finally, I always use real Scotch for a pure butterscotch flavor. Just don't waste a top-shelf Scotch on this recipe. Use a mid-level Scotch for the pudding and save the good stuff for drinking on the side. —JS

9 large egg yolks

2 cups half-and-half

2 cups (15.25 ounces/434 grams) packed light brown sugar

2 cups heavy cream

⅓ cup Scotch

1 tablespoon pure vanilla extract or vanilla bean paste

Whipped cream, for garnish

1. In a medium bowl, combine the egg yolks with 1 cup of the half-and-half and whisk until combined. Set aside.

2. In a large saucepan, combine the remaining 1 cup half-and-half, sugar, and cream and heat over medium-low heat, stirring occasionally, until the sugar has dissolved, about 5 minutes. (Do not let the mixture come to a boil or it will curdle.) Remove the pan from the heat.

3. Gradually whisk ½ cup of the warm cream mixture into the egg yolk mixture to temper the yolks. Slowly whisk the tempered yolks into the remaining cream mixture. Strain the liquid through a fine-mesh sieve into a medium bowl. Stir in the Scotch and vanilla. Cover the bowl with plastic wrap and refrigerate for 8 hours or overnight.

4. Arrange a rack in the center of the oven and preheat the oven to 350°F. Divide the chilled cream mixture among eight 6-ounce ramekins and place them in a roasting pan. Pour hot water into the pan to come halfway up the sides of the ramekins. Cover the dish with aluminum foil and poke holes in the top to create small air vents and let steam escape.

5. Bake the puddings for 50 minutes or until set in the center. To check the puddings for doneness, remove the foil and jiggle them gently. They should be completely set. If the puddings are not completely set, replace the foil and return the puddings to the oven to bake for 10 minutes more before testing them again.

6. Remove the baking pan from the oven and remove the foil. Let the puddings cool in the water bath until they are at room temperature, about 1 hour. Cover the puddings individually with plastic wrap and refrigerate until well chilled, about 3 hours. Dig in, with a generous spoonful of whipped cream.

Butterscotch Chip Cookies with Cream Cheese Frosting and Smoky Bacon

Makes 24 cookies and about 1 cup frosting

I first made these cookies when I was searching for a way to incorporate Adam's Smoky Bacon (page 62) into a dessert for the nose-to-tail culinary competition, Cochon 555. The salt in the bacon garnish balances out the sweetness of the butterscotch chips so the cookies aren't at all cloying. And though there are a few steps to make these cookies, the effort is totally worth it. They are always a hit. These cookies are best the day they are made. —JS

Butterscotch Chip Cookies

2¼ cups (11.25 ounces/324 grams) all-purpose flour

¾ teaspoon kosher salt

½ teaspoon baking powder

½ teaspoon baking soda

1 cup (2 sticks) unsalted butter, at room temperature

¾ cup (5.5 ounces/157 grams) packed light brown sugar

¾ cup (5.25 ounces/150 grams) granulated sugar

2 large eggs

1 teaspoon pure vanilla extract or vanilla bean paste

1¼ cups butterscotch chips

4 thick-cut bacon slices, cut into ¼ by 1-inch strips

Cream Cheese Frosting

1 (8-ounce) package cream cheese, at room temperature

6 tablespoons unsalted butter, at room temperature

⅓ cup (1.4 ounces/40 grams) confectioners' sugar

1 teaspoon pure vanilla extract or vanilla bean paste

½ teaspoon freshly squeezed lemon juice

1. **Make the butterscotch chip cookies:** In a medium bowl, combine the flour, salt, baking powder, and baking soda and whisk to combine. Set aside. In the bowl of a stand mixer fitted with the paddle attachment or in a bowl using a hand mixer, cream together the butter, brown sugar and granulated sugar on high speed until light and fluffy, 2 to 3 minutes.

2. Scrape down the sides of the bowl with a rubber spatula, then with the mixer running on medium speed, add the eggs, one at a time, and mix until combined. Add the vanilla and mix to combine. Add the flour mixture and mix to combine. Reduce the speed to low, add the butterscotch chips, and mix until just combined. Turn the dough out onto a sheet of plastic wrap and wrap tightly. Let the dough rest in the refrigerator for at least 30 minutes or up to 1 week.

3. Arrange racks in the upper and lower thirds of the oven and preheat the oven to 350°F. Line two large baking sheets with parchment paper.

4. Remove the cookie dough from the refrigerator and scoop mounds of the dough, roughly 2 tablespoons in size, onto the prepared baking sheets, placing the cookies about 1½ inches apart. Bake the cookies, rotating the baking sheets halfway through, for 10 to 12 minutes or until just golden on the edges but still soft in the middle. Remove the cookies from the oven and let cool on the baking sheets for 10 minutes. Transfer the cookies to a wire rack to cool completely.

5. Meanwhile, line a small plate with paper towels. In a medium skillet, cook the bacon over medium heat, stirring occasionally, until just crispy but still chewy, about 5 minutes. Remove the skillet from the heat and use a slotted spoon to transfer the bacon to the paper towel–lined plate and set aside.

6. **Meanwhile, make the cream cheese frosting:** In the bowl of a stand mixer fitted with the paddle attachment, combine the cream cheese and butter and mix on medium speed to combine. Add the confectioners' sugar, vanilla, and lemon juice and mix until combined, about 1 minute. Raise the speed to high and mix until the frosting is light and fluffy, about 3 minutes more. Transfer the frosting to a pastry bag fitted with a medium star tip and set aside.

7. Looking at the top of each cookie like a clock, start at the 12 o'clock position and pipe a mounded spiral design with the cream cheese frosting in the center of each cookie. Garnish the cookies with the bacon and dig in.

Arnie Palmer Popsicles

Makes about 10 pops

You'll often find me drinking Arnold Palmers in the summertime. One year, I decided to turn the refreshing drink into a nice, palate-cleansing sorbet. I thought it would be especially good after eating a plate of Adam's Skillet-Fried Chicken (page 156), and I was right. The sorbet was a hit! I then took the sorbet one step further and made Arnie Palmer popsicles.

You can use any shape and size of ice pop mold to make these. (Just be sure to extend the freezing time.) However, I like to make them using little Dixie cups and small popsicle sticks to serve as a fun, nostalgic dessert at parties. —JS

2 cups Simple Syrup (page 271), chilled

1 cup homemade iced tea, such as Lipton, chilled

1 cup freshly squeezed lemon juice, chilled

1. In a medium bowl, combine the simple syrup, iced tea, and lemon juice and whisk to combine.

2. On a large baking sheet, arrange ten Dixie cups in rows. Divide the mixture among the cups, filling each one three-quarters full. Cover the cups individually with plastic wrap. Using the tip of a paring knife, make a tiny cut, about ¼ inch wide, into the center of the plastic wrap above each cup. Gently insert a popsicle stick into each hole.

3. Transfer the baking sheet to the freezer and let the pops freeze completely, at least 8 hours or overnight. (You may want to check on them after 1 hour to see if any of the sticks have tilted. If so, make sure that the liquid is slightly frozen and then adjust the stick so it stands upright again.)

4. Once the popsicles have chilled, tear off the Dixie cup and serve, or store in the freezer for up to 1 month.

Birthday Cake

Makes 1 (8-inch) double-layer cake and about 4 cups frosting

This is my go-to chocolate birthday cake and frosting. It's dark. It's rich. And the frosting puts it over the top. You'll want to eat this frosting with a spoon.

This is the two-layer version of the cake. You can also cut the rounds in half to make it a four-layer cake. Then the cake really becomes a binder for all that frosting. You can make the frosting ahead of time and refrigerate it. Just be sure to take it out so it has enough time to come to room temperature when you're ready to use it. Before icing the cake, beat the frosting in a stand mixer fitted with the paddle attachment for 1 minute to refresh it. —JS

Chocolate Cake

⅓ cup plus 1 tablespoon unsalted butter, cut into ½-inch cubes

1 cup brewed dark-roast coffee, hot

1⅓ cups (6.7 ounces/192 grams) all-purpose flour

1 cup (4 ounces/114 grams) unsweetened Dutch-process cocoa powder

1 cup (7 ounces/200 grams) granulated sugar

2 teaspoons baking soda

1 teaspoon baking powder

1 cup low-fat buttermilk

4 large eggs, lightly beaten

Chocolate Frosting

10 large egg yolks (about ¾ cup)

2⅓ cups (9 ounces/257 grams) confectioners' sugar

1¼ teaspoons kosher salt

1¼ teaspoons pure vanilla extract or vanilla bean paste

5 tablespoons (1.25 ounces/36 grams) unsweetened Dutch-process cocoa powder

½ cup plus 2 tablespoons boiling water

2⅓ cups (10 ounces/285 grams) semisweet chocolate chips

1¼ cups (2½ sticks) unsalted butter

1. **Make the chocolate cake:** Arrange a rack in the center of the oven and preheat the oven to 350°F. Grease two 8-inch round cake pans and line them with parchment paper circles cut to fit.

2. In a small bowl, combine the butter with the hot coffee. Stir until the coffee melts the butter completely. Set aside.

3. In a large bowl, combine the flour, cocoa powder, granulated sugar, baking soda, and baking powder. Add the buttermilk and eggs and whisk to make a thick paste. Add the butter-coffee mixture and whisk until smooth. Divide the batter between the prepared cake pans. (The batter should come about two-thirds up the sides of the pans.) Tap the pans on the countertop to settle the batter.

4. Bake for 25 to 30 minutes or until a tester stick inserted into the center of the cakes comes out clean. Remove the cakes from the oven and let cool in the pans for 10 minutes. Turn the cakes out onto wire racks and let cool completely, about 1 hour. Once cooled, wrap the cakes in plastic wrap and put them in the freezer for 1 hour or in the refrigerator for 1 hour 30 minutes to chill before frosting. (This will make it easier to frost the cake because you'll have fewer crumbs to deal with.)

5. **Make the chocolate frosting:** In the bowl of a stand mixer fitted with the paddle attachment, combine the egg yolks, confectioners' sugar, salt, and vanilla and mix on high speed until thick and smooth, about 1 minute. Turn off the mixer and let the ingredients rest in the bowl.

6. In a small bowl, combine the cocoa powder with the boiling water and whisk until the cocoa powder dissolves. Set aside. Put the chocolate chips in a small bowl. In a small saucepan set over medium heat, warm the butter until it melts and gets hot. Pour the hot butter over the chocolate chips and whisk until they melt. Set aside.

7. Add the cocoa powder mixture to the yolk-sugar mixture and mix on medium speed to combine. Add the chocolate-butter mixture, raise the speed to medium-high, and mix until the frosting thickens and is cool and smooth, about 15 minutes.

8. Remove one of the cake layers from the freezer or refrigerator and put it on your cake stand. (If your cake round is slightly mounded, use a serrated knife to cut off the dome so the top is level.) Using a long, flexible spatula, take a large dollop of the frosting and spread it evenly over the top of the cake. Unwrap the second layer, trim it if needed, then place it cut-side down on top of the frosting on the first cake layer. (The bottom of the cake round will be the top of the cake.) Gently press down on the cake to help secure the layers, and make sure it is level.

9. Take another large dollop of frosting and spread it over the top of the cake. Take another dollop and holding your spatula vertically, spread the frosting along the sides of the cake. Rotate the cake and continue to spread the frosting along the side of the cake until it is completely covered with a thin layer of frosting.

10. Clean the spatula by running it under hot water. Dry it completely. Keeping your spatula vertical, gently smooth out the sides of the cake so you have a nice smooth frosted surface. (You may not need all the frosting. Stored in an airtight container in the refrigerator, it will keep for up to 2 weeks.) Using the spatula, smooth out the top and edges so the frosting on top of the cake is smooth as well. Decorate the cake as desired, then slice and celebrate.

THE BIRTHDAY CAKE

Birthday cakes are my quiet obsession. I got the bug from my nana, a true Renaissance woman, artist, and cake maker extraordinaire. Every year for my birthday, she and my grandpa would pull up in their 1977 VW camper, open the door, and reveal an amazing work of art sitting on the camper table. From a Raggedy Ann cake to one shaped like a guitar, Nana always delivered.

Now, as a pastry chef, I carry on my nana's cake tradition with my boys and the staff at the restaurant. They all up the ante every year, encouraging and challenging me to make a more ambitious cake. (There have been fudgy birthday cakes, R-rated cakes, and ones shaped like trains, soccer jerseys, dragons, and Ferraris.)

When you've made as many birthday cakes as I have, you develop a schedule that allows you to deliver. When a birthday is coming up, I use the party date as a deadline to get the cake parts ready for "the grand day of assembly." I always start by baking the cake a few days ahead. (You can cool the cake, wrap it in plastic wrap, and refrigerate it to keep it fresh; a chilled cake is also easier to frost and carve into intricate shapes.) I often gather decorations and make the frosting a day ahead of time as well.

When assembly day comes, I bring the frosting to room temperature, and rewhip it in the stand mixer to ensure that it spreads easily. If I'm making a layered cake, I use a serrated knife to slice the layers to the desired thickness, then frost in between the layers with an offset spatula. (I also slice layers in the sheet cakes I carve into unique shapes; frosting the layers keeps the cake moist.) Once I've frosted the cake, I start the real fun: the finer detail decorating.

I prefer to use frosting instead of fondant when decorating a cake. It just tastes better. Buy a decorating kit that has an assortment of frosting tips so you can try them out and learn to make great designs on your cake. If I do use fondant, I put a thick coat of frosting on the cake before I lay the rolled fondant over it, so when it's time to eat, I can peel off the fondant and eat the cake. (You can find fondant at craft stores or specialty cake-decorating stores.)

I like to purchase cake boxes for my cakes because it makes the cake feel like a present when it comes time to unveil my creation. The number of candles the birthday boy or girl puts on their special cake can be left up to them. —JS

MUDDLED, SHAKEN, AND STIRRED

The clink of ice cubes in a glass signals the time for refreshment and relaxation. In many cases, the cocktail hour is a time to stop our day-to-day hustle and catch up with the people who matter most. The drinks we love best for this purpose are inspired by classic cocktails like mint juleps or mimosas. The bartenders at The Country Cat have really honed the flavors of this collection of cocktails; they use quality spirits, infusions, fresh herbs, and freshly squeezed citrus juices to create refreshing, well-balanced cocktails that let you toss back a few without killing your taste buds. —AS and JS

Proud Mary

Makes 6 cocktails

We like to think of this big old Bloody Mary as a first course for brunch. We serve it up in pint-size mugs garnished with housemade Beef Jerky (page 124) and a garden of pickled vegetables. You can serve your Bloody Marys with or without these garnishes at home, but don't skip the salted rim. The spiced rimming salt gives this drink a great kick. —AS and JS

1 (46-ounce) can tomato juice

⅓ cup Worcestershire sauce

1½ tablespoons creamed horseradish

1 tablespoon freshly squeezed lemon juice

1 tablespoon ground celery seed

1 tablespoon lemon pepper

1 tablespoon freshly ground black pepper

8 dashes Tabasco sauce

2 tablespoons Bloody Mary Rimming Salt (opposite)

6 lime wedges, plus more for garnish

2 cups vodka

1. In a large pitcher, combine the tomato juice, Worcestershire, horseradish, lemon juice, celery seed, lemon pepper, black pepper, and Tabasco and stir until combined. Refrigerate for at least 2 hours or up to overnight.

2. Spread the rimming salt out on a small plate. Take a lime wedge and make a small slice in the middle; wet the rim of the glass with the lime wedge and dip the rim in the salt to coat. Fill the glass halfway with small ice cubes, then repeat with the remaining glasses.

3. Add the vodka to the pitcher with the tomato juice mixture and stir to combine. Divide the Proud Mary among the glasses. Garnish each glass with a lime wedge and any desired accompaniments and drink up.

Bloody Mary Rimming Salt

Makes about ½ cup

5 tablespoons kosher salt

1 tablespoon ground celery seed

1 tablespoon lemon pepper

1 tablespoon sweet paprika

In a small bowl, combine the salt, celery seed, lemon pepper, and paprika and whisk to combine. Transfer to an airtight container and store at room temperature until ready to use.

Good Morning Sunshine

Makes 1 cocktail

Our longtime bartender Jessie Matthews invented this hair-of-the-dog hangover cure to serve for New Year's Day brunch. The drink is packed with citrusy flavors. Even though you're imbibing when you toss back this fizzy cocktail, you feel like you're doing yourself some good because of the Emergen-C. —AS and JS

1½ ounces blood orange vodka, such as Indio Blood Orange Vodka

½ ounce orange liqueur, such as Patrón Citrónge

½ ounce freshly squeezed orange juice

¼ ounce freshly squeezed lemon juice

½ ounce Honey Simple Syrup (opposite)

1 teaspoon orange Emergen-C (about ½ packet)

Soda water, chilled

Orange wedge, for garnish

1. In a cocktail shaker, combine the blood orange vodka, orange liqueur, orange juice, lemon juice, simple syrup, and Emergen-C. Top the mixture with small ice cubes and shake vigorously.

2. Pour the cocktail into a highball glass or stemless wineglass and top with soda water to fill. Garnish with the orange wedge and drink up.

Honey Simple Syrup

Makes about 1½ cups

This honey simple syrup has a more round, nuanced sweetness than simple syrup made with sugar. Since honey and citrus go really well together, we use it in place of traditional syrup in citrusy cocktails like our Good Morning Sunshine (opposite). It's also great for sweetening a pitcher of iced tea. —AS and JS

1 cup honey

In a small saucepan set over low heat, combine the honey with 1 cup water and cook, stirring often, until the honey dissolves, about 5 minutes. Pour the syrup into a glass jar, let cool to room temperature, and store in the refrigerator for up to 1 month.

Proud Mary, page 266

Harvest Mimosa, page 270

The Maple Leaf

Makes 1 cocktail

When the leaves on Portland's many maple trees start changing color in the fall, we know it's time to put this cocktail back on our bar menu. In it, we pay homage to the great, widely available Pendleton Whisky that's made in our home state. You can use whatever Canadian whiskey you prefer and drink the cocktail cold or add hot water (see Bartender's Note) for a toddylike beverage to warm you up on a crisp fall day. —AS and JS

1¾ ounces Canadian whiskey, such as Pendleton

½ ounce pure maple syrup

¼ ounce freshly squeezed lemon juice

Lemon twist, for garnish

1. In a cocktail shaker, combine the whiskey, maple syrup, and lemon juice. Fill the shaker with ice cubes and shake to combine.

2. Strain into a martini glass. Garnish with the lemon twist and drink up.

Bartender's Note: To make a warm version of this cocktail, combine the whiskey with the maple syrup and lemon juice in a mug or tea glass and top with 1 to 1½ cups hot water. Stir, then garnish with the lemon twist and drink up.

Harvest Mimosa

Makes 1 cocktail

This fall spin on a classic mimosa uses fresh-pressed apple cider along with a shot of apple brandy and a dash of bitters in a sparkling cocktail that's perfect for brunch. We like the apple brandy from Portland's Clear Creek Distillery but you can use any high quality apple brandy you like. —AS and JS

1 ounce apple brandy, such as Clear Creek

1 ounce unfiltered unsweetened apple cider, chilled

2 dashes old-fashioned bitters, such as Peychaud's

Sparkling wine or Champagne, chilled

1 whole star anise

In a Champagne flute, combine the brandy, apple cider, and bitters and stir to combine. Top with sparkling wine to fill the flute and pop a star anise in the glass. Drink up.

The Kentucky Housewife

Makes 1 cocktail

We created this play on a mint julep with a Kentucky girl in mind. It's a sweet and minty bourbon cocktail that gets a bit of fizz from the soda water. Drink it on a sunny day outside on a porch, if you can. —AS and JS

10 fresh mint leaves, plus a sprig of fresh mint for garnish

1½ ounces bourbon, such as Bulleit

1 ounce Simple Syrup (opposite)

½ cup soda water, chilled

1. In a pint glass, combine the mint with enough small ice cubes to fill the glass three-quarters full. Using a muddler, muddle the ice and mint until the ice is broken up and the mint is in small pieces.

2. Add the bourbon and simple syrup to the glass and use a cocktail shaker to shake like crazy for 15 seconds. Pour the cocktail into a tall Collins glass and top with the soda water. Garnish with a mint sprig and drink up.

Simple Syrup

Makes about 1½ cups

1 cup sugar

In a small saucepan, combine the sugar with 1 cup water and cook over low heat, stirring often, until the sugar dissolves, about 2 minutes. Pour the syrup into a glass jar, let cool to room temperature, and store in the refrigerator for up to 1 month.

El Gato Verde

Makes 1 cocktail

Cooling celery and muddled cilantro give this spin on the classic margarita its clean flavor and green tint. (The name means "the green cat.") They go down easy, especially on a hot summer day. —AS and JS

½ medium celery stalk, peeled, trimmed, and cut into ½-inch pieces (see Chef's Note, page 93)

¼ cup fresh cilantro leaves

1½ ounces mid-range tequila, such as Sauza Hornitos

1 ounce freshly squeezed orange juice

¾ ounce freshly squeezed lime juice

½ ounce orange liqueur, such as Patrón Citrónge

½ ounce Simple Syrup (page 271)

Kosher salt

Lime wedge, for the rim

Lime wheel, for garnish

1. In a cocktail shaker, combine the celery with the cilantro. Fill the container three-quarters full with small ice cubes. Using a muddler, muddle the celery, cilantro, and ice until the celery and cilantro are in small pieces.

2. Add the tequila, orange juice, lime juice, orange liqueur, and simple syrup to the shaker and shake vigorously.

3. Spread some salt out on a small plate. Wet the rim of a highball glass with the lime wedge and dip the rim in the salt to coat. Fill the glass with ice cubes. Strain the cocktail into the glass and garnish with the lime wedge. Drink up.

The Ginger Lee

Makes 1 cocktail

Infused Ginger Vodka lends our version of a Lemon Drop more pep than the original. We like to think it's the kind of cocktail a Midwest gal would sip while passing time on a hot day. –AS and JS

1½ ounces house-infused Ginger Vodka (opposite)

½ ounce limoncello

½ ounce Simple Syrup (page 271)

½ ounce freshly squeezed lemon juice

Sugar

Lemon wedge

Candied ginger, for garnish

1. In a cocktail shaker, combine the ginger vodka, limoncello, simple syrup, and lemon juice. Fill the shaker with ice cubes and shake to combine.

2. Spread some sugar out on a small plate. Use the lemon wedge to wet the rim of a martini glass and dip the rim in the sugar to coat. Strain the cocktail into the glass. Garnish with the candied ginger on a toothpick and drink up.

Ginger Vodka

Makes 1 (750-ml) bottle

Few infused spirits are as quick and easy to make as this ginger vodka. Use it to spike iced tea or lemonade or in our favorite summer cocktail: the Ginger Lee (opposite). When you're infusing the vodka, make sure you save the vodka bottle so you can pour the infusion back into it to store. —AS and JS

¼ pound fresh ginger

1 (750-ml) bottle mid-range vodka, such as Monopolowa

1. In the bowl of a food processor fitted with the steel blade, pulse the ginger until it forms a chunky puree. (You should have about ½ cup.) Pour the vodka into a large glass container or pitcher, add the ginger puree, and stir to combine. Cover the container with plastic wrap and refrigerate for 2 days to infuse the vodka.

2. Strain the ginger out of the vodka and transfer the vodka to a bottle. Stored in the refrigerator, the infused vodka will keep for up to 1 month.

Holiday Punch

Makes about 9½ cups

During holiday gatherings, it's nice to have a ready-made drink like this fizzy, citrusy punch on hand so you can spend time being social, not mixing drinks, when the party starts. You can make the cocktail in a pitcher ahead of time, then pour it into a punch bowl and add the soda water and ice just before guests arrive. —AS and JS

1 (750-ml) bottle cranberry vodka, chilled, such as Smirnoff

1¾ cups freshly squeezed orange juice (from 7 to 8 oranges), chilled

½ cup cranberry juice cocktail, chilled

1 tablespoon freshly squeezed lime juice

1 tablespoon Grenadine (opposite)

3 cups soda water, chilled

Orange wheels, for garnish

In a large pitcher, mix the vodka, orange juice, cranberry juice cocktail, lime juice, and grenadine and stir to combine. Pour the mixture into a large punch bowl filled with large ice cubes. Add the soda water. Serve in stemless wine glasses, garnished with an orange wheel.

Grenadine

Makes 4 cups

Once you make your own grenadine, you'll never go back to drinking overly sweet commercial versions of this pomegranate syrup. Homemade grenadine has a much cleaner flavor that goes great with Champagne and bourbon, as well as our Holiday Punch (opposite). —AS and JS

4 cups sugar

4 cups pomegranate juice

In a medium saucepan, combine the sugar with the pomegranate juice and bring to a boil. Reduce the heat to maintain a hard simmer and cook until reduced by one-third, about 10 minutes. Pour the grenadine into a glass jar, let cool to room temperature, and store in the refrigerator for up to 1 month.

BOURBON FOR BREAKFAST

In the summer, we spend many of our weekends camping. During those quiet mornings at our campsite, we often wake up with a campfire, cast-iron eggs and bacon, French press coffee, and a snicker of bourbon to top it off. Having a little bourbon for breakfast helps start the day off nice and easy.

There's something about bourbon that suits a slow, lazy morning, and when you think about the long, slow process that goes into making it, it makes sense. Early Americans in Bourbon County, Kentucky, took the region's sweet corn, mixed it with water, and let it sit and age in barrels while traveling down the Ohio River to Mississippi. The trip down the river gave the spirit time to turn a lovely amber color, come of age, and smooth out; to this day, bourbon is made in much the same way.

The aging process used to make bourbon gives the spirit sweet and savory qualities that make it a natural match for breakfast food. (These qualities are also why a bourbon cocktail for breakfast often leads to an afternoon sipping more bourbon on the porch swing.) Good bourbon can bring out the sweetness in maple syrup, heighten the taste of well-cured bacon, and round out the creamier qualities of slow-cooked grits.

One of our favorite brunch cocktails, our Cowboy Coffee, pays tribute to the bourbon mornings we enjoy in the woods. The restaurant's rendition includes a shot of espresso in the mug to give the coffee an extra kick. The drink lets diners bite the hair of the dog and jump-start their day at the same time—slowly. For a crazy twist on a mimosa, mix bourbon with sparkling rosé and top with orange soda, such as Clementine Izze, and it's sunshine in a glass. —AS and JS

Bread-and-Butter Pickles, page 280

PICKLED AND PRESERVED

There is a visceral satisfaction that happens after you've cooked, processed, pickled, or preserved a fruit or vegetable in its prime. These traditions and practices were developed to capture the freshness of produce at its peak so you can relive the experience of eating it long after the season has passed. Months later, when you break the seal and hear that pop of a lid opening, it's like discovering a time capsule that reminds you of the flavors of a fall harvest or of how good summer berries tasted when the sun was shining and the air was warm. —AS and JS

Bread-and-Butter Pickles

Makes 6 pint jars

Soaking vegetables in cold water overnight before plunging them into a brine tightens their cell structure and helps them stay crisp longer. When prepping the peppers, leave the stems on so they are easy to remove from the jar. Bring a batch of these classic pickles on a picnic or serve them on the side of Judy (page 118) or with BBQ foods. —AS

6 small carrots, trimmed and peeled

6 pickling cucumbers, such as Kirby cucumbers, quartered lengthwise

6 small sweet chile peppers, such as Lipstick peppers, halved lengthwise and seeded

3 large cauliflower florets, halved

3 small fennel bulbs, quartered

3 cups apple cider vinegar

2½ cups packed light brown sugar

6 garlic cloves, smashed

3 star anise

1 cinnamon stick

1½ tablespoons kosher salt

1½ teaspoons freshly ground black pepper

1½ teaspoons ground celery seed

1½ teaspoons coriander seed

1½ teaspoons fennel seed

1½ teaspoons yellow mustard seed

1½ teaspoons ground turmeric

1. In a large bowl or plastic tub, combine the carrots, cucumbers, chile peppers, cauliflower, and fennel bulbs. Pour 10 cups ice water over the vegetables to cover and put a plate on the top to submerge them. Cover the container with plastic wrap and refrigerate to soak overnight.

2. The next day, in a medium saucepan, combine 3 cups water, the vinegar, sugar, garlic, star anise, cinnamon stick, salt, pepper, celery seed, coriander seed, fennel seed, mustard seed, and turmeric. Bring the brine to a simmer over medium heat, then cook at a low simmer for 5 minutes to let the flavors blend.

3. Pour the brine into a large nonreactive pan and let it cool completely, about 1 hour. When the brine is cool, remove the vegetables from the refrigerator and drain. Pack the vegetables into six sterilized 1-pint jars, dividing them equally, and pour the brine over the vegetables. Cover the jars tightly with lids and refrigerate for at least 1 week or up to 1 month before eating.

Dried Fruit Compote

Makes 5 (8-ounce) jars

Summer provides a glut of fresh fruit to make seasonal compotes for the breakfast table. Winter, however, is a challenging season for fruit in many parts of the country, so I rely on dried fruits like cherries, currants, and raisins to create this comforting cold-weather compote. The gently spiced condiment has all the flavors of a great mulled wine and is as good spooned over Ridiculously Good Buttermilk Pancakes (page 46) and Challah French Toast (page 47) as it is used to garnish a bowl of ice cream for dessert. —JS

3 cups granulated sugar

2 cups dried sour cherries

1 cup currants

1 cup golden raisins

2 cinnamon sticks

½ vanilla bean, split and seeds scraped

1 orange, halved

2 cups dry red wine, such as Syrah

1. In a medium saucepan, combine the sugar, cherries, currants, raisins, cinnamon sticks, vanilla bean pod, and vanilla bean seeds. Juice the orange halves into the pan. Add 1 juiced orange half to the pan and discard the remaining half. Add the wine and 2 cups water and bring the mixture to a strong simmer over medium heat. Simmer, stirring occasionally, until the sugar has dissolved and the fruit is plump, about 10 minutes.

2. Remove the pan from the heat and drain the dried fruit, reserving the liquid. Discard the cinnamon sticks, vanilla bean pod, and orange half and set the dried fruit aside. Return the liquid to the pan and cook over medium-low heat until it is slightly syrupy and has reduced by half, about 30 minutes. (The syrup will thicken a bit more as it cools.)

3. Pour the reduced syrup over the dried fruit and stir to combine. Serve the compote warm or let cool to room temperature and transfer to an airtight container. Stored in the refrigerator, the compote will keep for up to 5 days, though you can also preserve it in sterilized glass jars to extend its shelf life, if you wish. (Reheat the compote on the stovetop over low heat before serving.)

Smoked Tomato Jam

Makes 7 (8-ounce) jars

Years ago, when I was looking for a condiment that could stand the test of every season, I spotted a recipe for tomato jam in a book called *Cured* by Lindy Wildsmith. The original recipe is phenomenal and has inspired many iterations in my kitchen, including this smoked version. I'd call it the ultimate condiment: It has nice acid and is sour, sweet, and spicy at once. It's also good on everything from lamb burgers to roast chicken to grilled cheese sandwiches. In the spring, I add a few tablespoons of finely chopped mint to the jam, and in the fall, I toss in some finely chopped fresh sage just before taking it off the stove.

If you don't have access to a smoker, you can skip step 1 to make this tomato jam with plain canned tomatoes and still get great results. —AS

1 cup hickory chips, for smoking

3 (28-ounce) cans whole peeled tomatoes, preferably San Marzano, with their juices

2 dried pasilla chiles

2 cups packed light brown sugar

2 cups granulated sugar

¼ cup finely grated peeled fresh ginger

4 garlic cloves, finely chopped

Finely grated zest of 2 lemons

1. Soak the hickory chips according to the package instructions and preheat a smoker to 225°F. (Or see "Smoking Without a Smoker," page 35.) Place the wet hickory chips over the fire or in an electric hopper. Place the tomatoes in a stainless-steel, nonreactive roasting pan and smoke for 2 hours. Set aside. (This step can be done a day ahead.)

2. Fill a medium saucepan with water and add the chiles. Cover the saucepan and bring to a simmer over medium heat. Cook the chiles until tender, about 15 minutes. Drain the chiles and transfer to a cutting board to cool slightly. Using a sharp knife, remove the stems, veins, and seeds. Transfer the chiles to the bowl of a food processor fitted with the steel blade and puree.

3. In a large Dutch oven, combine the smoked tomatoes, the puree, brown sugar, granulated sugar, ginger, garlic, and lemon zest and blend using a potato masher or your hands until combined. Bring the mixture to a simmer over medium-low heat and cook, stirring frequently with a wooden spoon and adjusting the heat as needed to prevent scorching, until the jam is thick and glossy, about 2 hours.

4. Remove the jam from the heat and transfer to an airtight container. Let cool to room temperature. Stored in the refrigerator, the jam will keep for up to 2 weeks, though you can also preserve it in sterilized glass jars to extend its shelf life, if you wish.

Summer Berry Jam

Makes about 5 (8-ounce) jars

When you combine a variety of fresh berries in a jam, you get the best properties of the different berries in each jar. (I also find that a mixed berry jam isn't as seedy as a single berry jam.) This summer preserve is great on toast and Buttermilk Biscuits (page 43) or swirled into ice cream. And it makes a thoughtful hostess gift.

Though fresh berries make the best jam, you can also use frozen berries in this recipe. If you use frozen fruit, don't worry about halving the strawberries and plan on cooking the berries slightly longer to account for the extra water they'll release. —JS

1 pound fresh or frozen blackberries

1 pound fresh or frozen blueberries

1 pound fresh or frozen raspberries

½ pound fresh or frozen strawberries, hulled and halved

3 cups sugar

Finely grated zest of 1½ lemons

¼ cup freshly squeezed lemon juice

1. In a large, nonreactive, heavy-bottomed stockpot or saucepan, combine the blackberries, blueberries, raspberries, strawberries, sugar, lemon zest, and lemon juice. Bring the mixture to a gentle simmer over medium-low heat, then stir to combine the fruit and incorporate and dissolve the sugar. Cook, stirring occasionally, for 40 minutes. (If the fruit starts to stick to the bottom of the pan, reduce the heat a bit to prevent scorching.)

2. Take a heaping spoonful of the jam and place it on a small plate. Place the plate in the freezer for 10 minutes. (Continue to cook and stir the jam in the stockpot over low heat in the meantime.) Remove the plate from the freezer and drag a finger through the jam. If the trail remains clean and the jam looks thick, the jam is done. If the jam still seems loose and watery, cook the jam, stirring occasionally, for 15 minutes more.

3. Remove the jam from the heat and divide it among five 8-ounce jars. Let cool to room temperature or have a batch of biscuits ready to slather with warm jam. Stored in an airtight container in the refrigerator, the jam will keep for up to 2 weeks, though you can also preserve it in sterilized glass jars to extend its shelf life, if you wish.

Apple Butter

Makes about 5 (8-ounce) jars

When autumn comes around, this spice-laden fruit butter becomes our go-to preserve to serve with buttery Buttermilk Biscuits (page 43). It's also great swirled into vanilla ice cream, if you're so inclined. Adding apple cider vinegar to the recipe ensures that the preserve isn't too sweet and that the apple flavor really pops. —JS

3 pounds good cooking apples, such as Braeburn or Gravensteins, peeled, cored, and cut into ¼- to ½-inch-thick slices

½ cup apple cider vinegar

Finely grated zest of 1 lemon

2 tablespoons freshly squeezed lemon juice

2½ cups sugar

1½ teaspoons ground cinnamon

¼ teaspoon ground cloves

¼ teaspoon ground ginger

1. In a large Dutch oven, combine the apples, 1½ cups water, the vinegar, lemon zest, and lemon juice. Bring the mixture to a boil over medium-high heat. Reduce the heat to medium-low and cook, stirring occasionally, until the apples are very soft, about 25 minutes.

2. Remove the Dutch oven from the heat and, using a potato masher, mash the apples until completely mashed. Add the sugar, cinnamon, cloves, and ginger and stir to combine. Return the mixture to the stovetop and cook over low heat, stirring frequently to prevent scorching, until very thick, about 30 minutes more. (The apple butter will thicken a bit more as it cools.)

3. Remove the Dutch oven from the heat and let the apple butter cool for 5 minutes. Working in batches, if needed, transfer the apple butter to the bowl of a food processor fitted with the steel blade and puree until smooth. Divide the apple butter among five 8-ounce jars. Let cool to room temperature. Stored in the refrigerator, the apple butter will keep for up to 2 weeks, though you can also preserve it in sterilized glass jars to extend its shelf life, if you wish.

PUTTIN' UP

The Los Angeles I grew up in wasn't a hotbed for canning and preserving. I always thought preserving was something grandmas did to pass the time. But when I moved to Oregon and experienced the state's four seasons and amazing bounty, I found myself wanting to try this age-old process. Only I was a bit intimidated by the scale of the whole thing. The recipes I found in books yielded large batches, but my apartment and budget were fairly small.

That's when I discovered that small-batch preserving is the way to go.

When you pickle and preserve fruits and vegetables in small batches, you get the best of both worlds. You can stock your pantry with enough jars to extend the season but not so many that you'll tire of a berry jam or bread-and-butter pickles by the time you work your way through your pantry stash. You'll also find the task of pickling or preserving to be more manageable, which means it will become a project you look forward to, not dread.

Whether I'm pickling cucumbers, carrots, or asparagus, I usually start with 10 pounds of each vegetable, which yields about six large jars. When I make jam, I like to visit a U-pick field with the boys. It's a great field trip and produces instant gratification when you leave with a lovely flat of ripe, plump berries or a bucket of apples. Or you can go to your local farmers' market and buy their bounty.

When you bring your stash home and tackle preserving on a smaller scale, you can start and finish most projects before noon. Then you have the rest of a beautiful day to relax but still get the satisfaction that you crafted something you can enjoy after the season has passed. —JS

Note: Page references in *italics* indicate recipe photographs.

A

Apple
  Butter, 286
  Green, and Smoky Bacon Ragout, Crispy Fried Oysters with, 144–45
  Pie, Free-Form, 240–42, *241*
Apple Cider and Brown Butter, Autumn Squash Soup with, 106–7
Arnie Palmer Popsicles, 258
Aromatics, cooking with, 30, 110
Arugula, Fennel, and Marjoram, Melon Salad with, 82, *83*
Asparagus
  Casserole, *214*, 215–16
  Morel and Spring Vegetable Hash, *60*, 61
  and Wild Rice Soup with Parsley Lemon Garlic Butter, *90*, 92–93
Avocados
  Green Goddess Dressing, 70–72

B

Bacon
  Pecan Spoonbread, 222–23, *223*
  Smoky, and Cream Cheese Frosting, Butterscotch Chip Cookies with, 256–57
  Smoky, and Green Apple Ragout, Crispy Fried Oysters with, 144–45
  Smoky, –Braised Collard Greens, 211
  Smoky, My, 62–63, *63*
  -Wrapped Trout with Summer Vegetables, *136*, 137–38
Baker's scale, 36

Balsamic-Braised Figs, Grilled Lamb Leg Steaks with, 193
Barley-Quinoa Cakes, 226–27
Basil-Infused Strawberry Shortcakes, 248–49, *250*
Bean(s)
  Chanterelle and Blackberry Succotash, 218, 219
  Green, Chanterelle, and Freekeh Salad with Huckleberry Vinaigrette, 73–75, *74*
  Mama's Chili, 108–9, *109*
  Pole, Olive Oil–Braised, *212*, 213
Beef
  Chicken-Fried Steak with "Woo" Gravy, 180–81
  Meat Candy (aka Beef Jerky), 124, *125*
  Mustard and Hazelnut Crusted Tri-Tip, 187
  Red Wine–Braised, with Wild Mushroom Steak Sauce, *182*, 183–84
Beets
  Crispy Pig's Ear Salad with Ranch Dressing, 84–85
Berry(ies)
  Basil-Infused Strawberry Shortcakes, 248–49, *250*
  Chanterelle and Blackberry Succotash, 218, *219*
  Huckleberry Vinaigrette, 73–75
  Summer, Jam, *285*, 287
Birthday Cake, 260–61, *263*
Biscuits, Buttermilk, *42*, 43–44
Blackberry(ies)
  and Chanterelle Succotash, 218, *219*
  Summer Berry Jam, *285*, 287
Blender, 36
Bloody Mary Rimming Salt, 266
Blue Cheese Buttermilk Dressing, 163

Bourbon
  Challah French Toast with Maker's Mark Custard and Clabber Cream, 47–48
  The Kentucky Housewife, 271
  Peach Crumble Pie, 236–37
  tasting notes, 277
Braising, 35
Brandy
  Harvest Mimosa, *269*, 270
  Wild Mushroom Steak Sauce, 183
Bread Pudding–Stuffed Lamb Shoulder, 195–96, *197*
Breads and stuffing
  Brioche Pecan Cinnamon Rolls, 54–55, *56*
  Buttermilk Biscuits, *42*, 43–44
  Challah Bread, *49*, 50–53
  Challah French Toast with Maker's Mark Custard and Clabber Cream, 47–48
  Cornbread Muffins, 78–79
  Granny Cris's Stuffing, 228–29
  Soft Buttery Pretzels, 116–17
Breakfast
  Breakfast Sausage with Maple Mustard, 64–65
  Brioche Pecan Cinnamon Rolls, 54–55, *56*
  Buttermilk Biscuits, *42*, 43–44
  Challah Bread, *49*, 50–53
  Challah French Toast with Maker's Mark Custard and Clabber Cream, 47–48
  Morel and Spring Vegetable Hash, *60*, 61
  My Smoky Bacon, 62–63, *63*
  Ridiculously Good Buttermilk Pancakes, 46
  Slow Burn, 57, 58–59
Brioche Pecan Cinnamon Rolls, 54–55, *56*

NOTES

NOTES

NOTES

NOTES

NOTES

NOTES

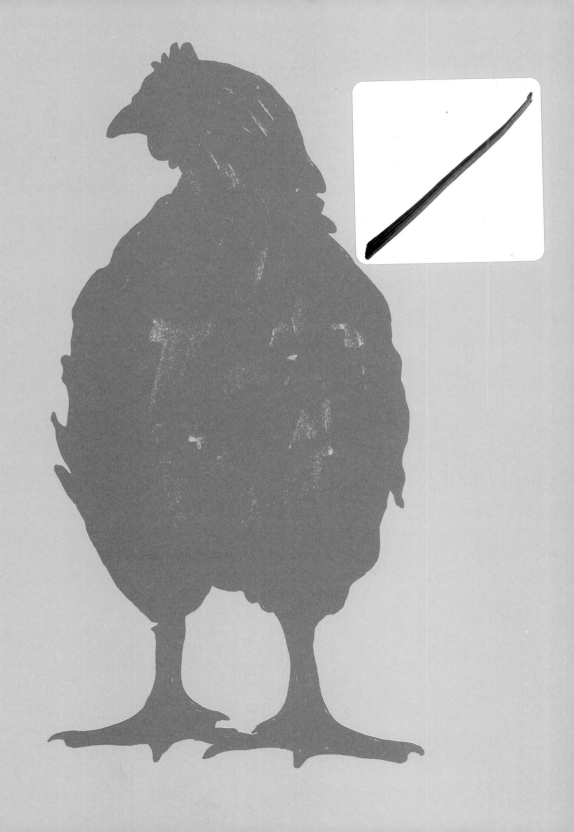